Chicago Bee Branch
3647 S. State Street
Chicago, IL 60609

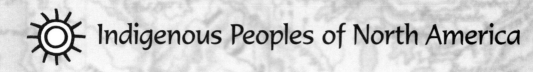
The Sioux

Titles in the Indigenous Peoples of North America Series Include:

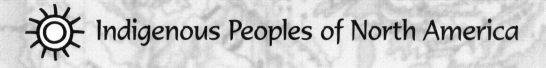

The Sioux

Gwen Remington

Lucent Books, Inc.
P.O. Box 289011, San Diego, California

To Brenda Griffing

Library of Congress Cataloging-in-Publication Data

Remington, Gwen, 1956 –
    The Sioux / by Gwen Remington.
       p.   cm. — (Indigenous peoples of North America series)
    Includes bibliographical references and index.
    Summary: Discusses the Native American tribe the Sioux, also known
as the Dakota, including their life on the American desert, social and
political organizational, customs, religion, and assimilation.
    ISBN 1-56006-615-6 (lib. bdg. : alk. paper)
    1. Dakota Indians—Juvenile literature. [1. Dakota Indians. 2.
Indians of North America—Great Plains.] I. Title. II. Series: Indigenous
peoples of North America.
  E99.D1 R36   2000
  978'.0049752—dc21   99-32703
                                                          CIP

Copyright 2000 by Lucent Books, Inc.
P.O. Box 289011, San Diego, California 92198-9011

Printed in the U.S.A.

Contents

Foreword

North America's native peoples are often relegated to history—viewed primarily as remnants of another era—or cast in the stereotypical images long found in popular entertainment and even literature. Efforts to characterize Native Americans typically result in idealized portrayals of spiritualists communing with nature or bigoted descriptions of savages incapable of living in civilized society. Lost in these unfortunate images is the rich variety of customs, beliefs, and values that comprised—and still comprise—many of North America's native populations.

The *Indigenous Peoples of North America* series strives to present a complex, realistic picture of the many and varied Native American cultures. Each book in the series offers historical perspectives as well as a view of contemporary life of individual tribes and tribes that share a common region. The series examines traditional family life, spirituality, interaction with other native and non-native peoples, warfare, and the ways the environment shaped the lives and cultures of North America's indigenous populations. Each book ends with a discussion of life today for the Native Americans of a given region or tribe.

In any discussion of the Native American experience, there are bound to be sim-

ilarities. All tribes share a past filled with unceasing white expansion and resistance that led to more than four hundred years of conflict. One U.S. administration after another pursued this goal and fought Indians who attempted to defend their homelands and ways of life. Although no war was ever formally declared, the U.S. policy of conquest precluded any chance of white and Native American peoples living together peacefully. Between 1780 and 1890, Americans killed hundreds of thousands of Indians and wiped out whole tribes.

The Indians lost the fight for their land and ways of life, though not for lack of bravery, skill, or a sense of purpose. They simply could not contend with the overwhelming numbers of whites arriving from Europe or the superior weapons they brought with them. Lack of unity also contributed to the defeat of the Native Americans. For most, tribal identity was more important than racial identity. This loyalty left the Indians at a distinct disadvantage. Whites had a strong racial identity and they fought alongside each other even when there was disagreement because they shared a racial destiny.

Although all Native Americans share this tragic history they have many distinct differences. For example, some tribes and individuals sought to cooperate almost immediately with the U.S. government while others steadfastly resisted the white presence. Life before the arrival of white settlers also varied. The nomads of the Plains developed altogether different lifestyles and customs from the fishermen of the Northwest coast.

Contemporary life is no different in this regard. Many Native Americans—forced onto reservations by the American government—struggle with poverty, poor health, and inferior schooling. But others have regained a sense of pride in themselves and their heritage, enabling them to search out new routes to self-sufficiency and prosperity.

The *Indigenous Peoples of North America* series attempts to capture the differences as well as similarities that make up the experiences of North America's native populations—both past and present. Fully documented primary and secondary source quotations enliven the text. Sidebars highlight events, personalities, and traditions. Bibliographies provide readers with ideas for further research. In all, each book in this dynamic series provides students with a wealth of information as well as launching points for further research.

A Migration from the Woods of Minnesota to the Upper Great Plains

The Sioux did not keep written records, so not much is known of their history before the 1600s, which is when the first white men began to trickle into their country. Their language is similar to that spoken by some tribes in eastern North America. Possibly the Sioux originated there and migrated west, eventually settling in what is now Minnesota. While exploring the area around Lake Superior in the seventeenth century, the French missionary Claude-Jean Allouez "heard . . . of the Sioux and their great river the 'Messipi.'"[1] By the time the first French fur traders arrived at the head of the Mississippi River, they found a large, loosely organized nation of seven tribes.

The French were curious about this fierce, warlike people. They asked the Algonquian Ojibwa, also known as the Chippewa, about them. The Ojibwa told the French that these seven tribes were called the Nadowe-is-iw, or "Lesser Adders." The French could not have chosen a worse tribe to ask. The Ojibwa considered the Sioux their enemies, second only to the Iroquois, whom they called "True Adders." An adder is a snake, and a lesser adder is a little snake—not an especially nice name in any language. The uncomplimentary name stuck and in time was shortened to the word *S-iw*, or *Sioux*.

Seven Council Fires

The Sioux had another name for their nation: Ociti Sakowin, which translates to "Seven Council Fires." The Seven Council Fires consisted of the four Santee, or Eastern, Sioux tribes (Mdewakanton, Wahpeton, Wahpekute, and Sisseton), who called themselves the Dakota; the Yankton and Yanktonai tribes, who called themselves the Nakota; and the Teton, or Western, Sioux tribe, who called themselves the Lakota. All three names—Dakota, Nakota, and Lakota—mean the same thing in the slightly different Sioux dialects: "allies."

And allies they were. When conditions permitted, these seven tribes met each summer for a great council. They also made a pledge that they would not attack one another. This was a significant pact because the Sioux culture was based on war, and it frequently attacked neighboring tribes. This vow of nonaggression, coupled with their shared language and origins, served to bind the seven allies into one large nation. Although each tribe would take a different road in the subsequent centuries, they nonetheless possessed similar customs, religion, and social and political organization.

It is the Lakota that receives most of the attention, though. This was the fearsome Teton tribe that fought so gamely during the Indian wars in the latter half of the nineteenth century. In the words of *Sioux Trail* author John Upton Terrell,

> The . . . Teton always have been, and always will be, the "picture Indians" of western history. They fully deserve the distinction. Physically, mentally, and morally they rank among the highest type of American Indians, and they are superior in these qualities to many tribes. As a warrior society they may not be compared to any other Indian peoples, with the possible exception of the Iroquois. As to courage and bravery they have no peers. As to color and beauty in their regalia, and complexity and drama in the social and religious ceremonials and ritual, they are unsurpassed. As to cohesiveness as a people, as to faith in themselves as

Woodland "Savages"

In 1680 explorer Louis Hennepin encountered a party of Sioux warriors on their way to avenge the death of a young warrior at the hands of the Miami tribe. Upon hearing that the Miami had left the area, the Sioux decided instead to kidnap Hennepin and his men. During his stay with these Dakotas, Hennepin learned a great deal about their culture. In his book *La Salle and the Discovery of the Great West*, Francis Parkman describes a Sioux hunting scene as it was later recounted by Hennepin.

"It was a wild scene, this camp of savages among whom as yet no traders had come and handiwork of civilization had found its way,—the tall warriors, some nearly naked, some wrapped in buffalo-robes, and some in shirts of dressed deer-skin fringed with hair and embroidered with dyed porcupine quills, war-clubs of stone in their hands, and quivers at their backs filled with stone-headed arrows; the squaws, cutting smoke-dried meat with knives of flint, and boiling it in rude earthen pots of their own making, driving away, meanwhile, with shrill cries, the troops of lean dogs, which disputed the meal with a crew of hungry children. The whole camp, indeed, was threatened with starvation. The three white men could get no food but unripe berries."

individuals, as to confidence in their capability to overcome all obstacles, all adversities, all enemies, and as egotists, they are incomparable.[2]

Quite often when people think of the Sioux, it is the Lakota that comes to mind.

Migration

The Lakota do not deserve all of the credit, however, for the expulsion of the Seven Council Fires from the woods of Minnesota. All of the Sioux made for uncomfortable neighbors, raiding and plundering as the whim took them. When the other woodland tribes received guns from the French and English fur traders in the early seventeenth century, they went on the offensive. By the middle of the seventeenth century, the Yankton, Yanktonai, and Teton had been driven south, and sometime after 1735 the four Santee tribes followed.

The first three of these tribes continued their migration by moving westward onto

A meeting of the seven Sioux tribes took place each summer with representatives vowing to halt attacks among tribes.

Life as a Woodland Indian

The life of the woodland Sioux was decidedly different from that of their nomad descendants. They lived in elm-bark lodges situated in permanent villages to which they returned after each raid or hunt. For transport, they used birch-bark canoes, rapidly navigating the wooded Minnesota terrain through its network of lakes, rivers, and streams. Hunting was done on foot, with the hunters chasing their prey and bringing it down with stone-headed arrows.

The buffalo was a major part of their diet. They also consumed large quantities of wild rice mixed with berries and served in birch-bark bowls. Fish was quite naturally another important food. Some, most notably the Santee, supplemented their diet by farming, cultivating corn.

the prairie expanses of what are now South Dakota and North Dakota. The Yankton settled on the rich land between the Big Sioux and Missouri Rivers, the Yanktonai headed north to central North Dakota, and the Teton found a home in the western Dakotas and Nebraska and in eastern Montana and Wyoming. Although the Santee remained for a while longer in Minnesota, the white invasion would in time force them westward as well.

This eviction from the woods of Minnesota to the prairies of the Great Plains proved incredibly fortuitous for the Sioux. Their migration occurred at a wonderfully fortunate time for inhabitants of the middle United States, a time when the white man's guns were traveling west and his horses northeast. Because of this, and because they possessed a native adaptability and were therefore extraordinarily receptive to change, the Sioux made, in two brief centuries, an astonishing evolutionary leap from poor woodland folks to mighty Plains Indians.

Chapter 1

Life on "the Great American Desert"

At the time of the Sioux migration, there were few white men on the Great Plains of North America. The first explorers were uninterested in the area, calling it "the Great American Desert" and deeming it uninhabitable. This desert is a wide strip of land running from Texas in the south to Canada in the north, bounded on the west by the Rockies and on the east by the Mississippi, the Sioux's old home. According to author Alvin M. Josephy Jr.,

> The Plains area consists generally of two types of country, a somewhat humid region of tall-grass prairies roughly east of the hundred meridian, where the rainfall averages from 20 to 40 inches annually, and a drier expanse of short-grass high plains, or steppes, farther west, where precipitation averages from 10 to 20 inches a year.[3]

The Sioux made their home in the northern section of these plains, a seemingly inhospitable country whose fertile eastern prairies now feed much of the modern United States. The northwestern steppes consist of barren plains broken by rock outcroppings and occasional mountain ranges. They are a hauntingly desolate country. In the center of these two areas, carving a route through the bleak Dakota Badlands, runs the Missouri River. To its immediate west are the Paha Sapa, the Sioux's sacred and much beloved Black Hills, a strikingly beautiful collection of wooded hills and massive rocks.

In the summer the grass-covered prairies were a magnet for game, and hunting was good. In the winter the river valleys and wooded hills provided shelter from the elements. The variety of terrain encouraged travel, and the Lakota became true nomads, moving their villages with the seasons and the availability of game and produce. The Nakota became seminomadic, returning to their established villages after hunts and raids. The resident Arikara and Mandan tribes, though reluctant to concede their territory to these interlopers, soon succumbed to both the Sioux and the deadly diseases carried on the breath and skin of the white man. After chasing the Crow from the sacred Black Hills, the Sioux took possession of the northern Great Plains.

The Climate of the Upper Great Plains

Their life was not easy. The northern Great Plains climate can be dangerous. Few regions in the United States claim as wide a range of temperatures, from minus thirty in the winters to over a hundred in the summer. Of even greater danger are the seasonal storms. In the early spring ice storms release torrents of springlike rain, and the earth, still in the grips of winter, freezes the rain as it lands, coating the landscape in thick layers of unrelenting ice. Trees, unable to support the weight of the ice, reluctantly shed their branches, and the sound of explosive cracking fills the air. Summer brings thunderstorms, and lightning rips the sky, thunder shakes the ground, and the clouds erupt, often with deadly hail. There are also tornadoes, whirling dervishes of two-hundred- to three-hundred-mile-per-hour winds that wreak a meandering path of destruction.

The most dangerous storm of all, though, comes with the arrival of winter:

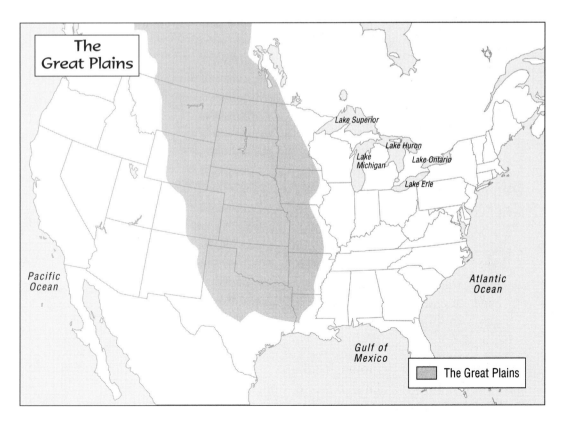

Winter Counts

The Sioux did not possess a written language. It is a great loss to the world that this fascinating culture did not leave a recorded history. However, they did leave something that, although not as precise as a written history, provides important records of their past: the winter count.

"The winter count was an *aide-memoire* in the form of colored pictographs painted on a buffalo robe, each picture representing the event by which that particular year, or 'winter' as the Sioux called it, was to be recalled," George E. Hyde writes in his *Red Cloud's Folks,* a study of the Oglala tribe. The pictograph selected to represent a particular year was one depicting the most notable event having occurred.

For example, the winter kill of large numbers of horses merited entry, much as did the death of an important leader or warrior. Incidents related to strange astronomical events, such as meteor showers and eclipses, were also recorded. Whether successful or unsuccessful, memorable battles with enemy tribes were often used to identify a year. Anything memorable would do, and the more easily recognizable, the better.

Some of the more important of these winter counts were made by the Yanktonai warrior Lone Dog and the Teton warriors The Flame, The Swan, Cloud Shield, and American Horse. Thanks to their winter counts and others, the world is not without at least some recorded history for the Sioux.

Recording the most important events of a particular year, winter counts give a partial history of the Sioux.

the northern Great Plains blizzard. First, temperatures drop to dangerous levels. Then heavy clouds move in. Gradually the wind rises. When the clouds dump their burden of snow, the howling wind delivers it in the form of tiny skin-battering arrowheads. A combination of wind and cold temperatures drives the temperature endured by exposed flesh—the windchill—to levels sufficient to cause frostbite within minutes. Even today the Great Plains blizzard can be deadly. Yet the Sioux, housed only in their tepees (sometimes spelled tipis), conical structures covered with buffalo hides, survived and even flourished in this climate.

After a blizzard passed, they would have emerged from these tepees and seen snowdrifts as tall as fifteen feet. The flat expanses of prairie would have been blanketed in a thick layer of brilliant snow, glittering so brightly in the sun that the Sioux would have been forced to look away. Much of this snow would remain until the spring thaw, restricting the Sioux to their winter camps for a third of each year. It is no wonder that the Sioux called years "winters" and recorded their yearly history with pictographs called "winter counts." Winter survival was a major part of life on the Great Plains.

The Great Plains: Horn of Plenty

The bounty of the land made up for its dangerous climate. Although the nomadic Lakota looked with disgust on farming, their diets did not suffer from a lack of produce. According to John Upton Terrell, they ate "wild buffalo berries, cherries, gooseberries, juneberries, strawberries, potatoes, turnips, onions, arrowleaf berries, artichokes, plums, nuts."[4] The women and children gathered these, preparing some for immediate eating and drying others. Some of the dried fruit was mixed with dried meat and fat to make the winter staple of pemmican. This was stored in parfleches, decorated bags made from hide, which the Lakota carried with them when the camp moved. Extra dried fruit was stored in caches—holes in the ground covered to prevent theft—in case the tribe passed that way again.

In addition to the plant life, the Great Plains provided food high in protein. There were numerous varieties of fowl, including ducks, geese, grouse, pigeons, and owls. Bird eggs were a delicacy, although goose eggs, suspected of causing a nasty, pus-filled sore, were avoided. The streams yielded trout, which were delicious when cooked in a leaf-lined pit. Turtles were a rare treat. Bears were an excellent source of fat, as was the porcupine, also prized for the quills used in decorating apparel and hide containers. The prairies teemed with rodents, including rabbits, squirrels, and prairie dogs. There were also badgers, nasty animals with lethal claws capable of ripping flesh to the bone. The Sioux subdued badgers by jumping on their backs, breaking them.

The major source of food for the Sioux, however, was drawn to the Great Plains by its buffalo grass, a tough, nutritious stalk

Buffalo supplied the Sioux with everything they needed to survive, including ample meat for food and hides for clothing and shelter.

standing as tall as a man when mature. When the prairie winds caressed the broad expanses of buffalo grass, they swayed and rippled, drawing to them the ungulates, those four-legged, hoofed mammals that roamed the Upper Great Plains. Deer, antelope, and elk grew fat on this nourishing grass. However, the Sioux could not base their diet on these animals. Their lightning agility made them difficult to kill by a hunter on foot who was armed only with a bow and arrow. Nor could the Sioux rely on the vegetation. Sometimes they reached a favorite berry haunt only to find its branches already stripped bare. And the rodents and fish were too small to

feed a family. Had the Sioux depended on any of these resources for food, they may have starved.

There was one other Great Plains ungulate, though, upon which the Sioux could depend. This ungulate traveled in sufficient numbers to feed a tribe. Indeed, one individual was large enough that a family could feast for days on its meat. Its hides were thick enough and large enough to keep the Sioux warm through the toughest of winters. Its passage through the high tangle of Plains grass had provided the routes the Sioux walked during their migration from Minnesota, and "the location of their settlements was almost solely determined by the proximity of sizable . . . herds."[5] This ungulate, the American Bison, represented life to the Sioux.

The American Bison

Accurately known as the American Bison, this ungulate is generally called a buffalo. Standing over six feet tall at the top of its hump, the buffalo is an unattractive beast covered with heavy "wool" over its massive head, hump, and forequarters. Short horns adorn its shaggy head, and small eyes peer out from beneath them. A bull buffalo weighs one ton and, when forced on the offensive, can do a significant amount of damage to the aggressor. The buffalo prefers to run when attacked, though, and as a herd animal, it runs with companions. Back in the mid-1800s, the buffalo traveled in herds miles long, and when they ran, the ground trembled. This habit of traveling in large numbers and its tendency to run in a straight line made it easier to hunt than any other game. Its huge size meant that the Sioux did not need to kill too many, either, to eat well.

The Sioux held a number of major hunts each year. One was usually held in mid-summer, which was a good time to process the kill. Hides taken from a summer hunt were often used to make tepee covers. The summer coat made a thinner hide, but the conditions for rapid drying were optimum. The meat could be more quickly dried, too. And because fruit was plentiful, the Sioux women were able to prepare the winter's store of pemmican. "Anticipation of future needs was an important aspect of summer camp activity," according to author Norman Bancroft-Hunt, "and the greater part of the work resulting from the hunt was in processing hides that would be finished later in the year."[6]

Another important hunt took place in the fall. That is when the buffalo gathered for their mating season. During this time, the buffalo massed in great herds that blackened the horizon for as far as the eye could see. With this many buffalo in one place, success was likely. Best of all, the buffalo had grown heavy winter coats. Hides taken from buffalo in the fall made warm robes and bedding for the coming winter. Meat taken during the brisk fall weather spoiled less quickly than in the summer.

Hunting Techniques

The Sioux had a number of hunting techniques. A favorite was the "pound." Once the scouts had located a large buffalo herd, they found a nearby cliff or other sudden drop-off in the terrain. The tribe formed a hidden line along the route between the drop-off and the herd, a wide V that came to an open point at the cliff top. Several hunters charged up behind the buffalo, frightening them toward the concealed lines. Once the first few buffalo were within the V, the Sioux jumped up from their hiding places, yelling to prevent them from turning to either side. Although the herd leaders soon saw they were in trouble, it was too late. The other buffalo, coming up rapidly from behind, forced the leaders and many more off the cliff. The

Fish Pits

The Sioux fish pit was a clever invention, not unlike the crockpot used today, though more primitive. First a hole was dug in the ground, with depth and diameter determined by the quantity of fish to be cooked. Perhaps a foot deep and eighteen inches wide would cook enough fish to feed a large family. A thick layer of leaves was arranged in the bottom of the pit and, as much as possible, around its sides.

After the fish were cleaned, they were nestled on this bed of leaves. On top of the fish was placed a layer of thick sticks, and on top of this was another layer of leaves. If the pit was dug to the right depth, there would only be an inch or two of pit sides left at this point. The cook covered this shallow hole with dirt, bringing the top of the pit level with the rest of the ground. A fire of sufficient size, one that would last at least an hour, was built on the top of the pit. When this fire was finished burning and nothing but embers remained, the fish were cooked.

All that remained was to extract the tender fish from the bottom of the pit and, using leaves as napkins, eat it while it was hot. Not only did fish cooked in this manner feed a family, but it also made delicious "take-out" meals for warriors on the go.

hunters hurried to the base of the cliff, where they clubbed to death any buffalo that survived the fall.

Another method involved the hunters draping themselves in animal skins and sneaking up on the herd. Buffalo have a terrific sense of smell, but their vision is poor. Once all the hunters were close to the herd, a signal was given. The silent bows sang with arrow after arrow, dropping several of the beasts before the rest knew they were in danger. This method of hunting took great stealth and self-discipline. Woe to the hunter who shot too soon, frightening the herd and denying his companions their opportunity!

The Sioux had a technique for winter hunting, too. When the snow lay mounded in huge drifts, the hunters donned snowshoes, a flat surface made of twigs spaced even distances apart in an oval frame. These shoes enabled the Sioux to walk on the snow without sinking in. The buffalo, with their sharp hooves and immense bulk, were not so fortunate. The hunters chased the buffalo on foot, guiding them into the deepest drifts. The ungainly beasts would flounder helplessly in the deep snow while the hunters took their time making the most accurate shots.

Utilizing the Carcass

The buffalo satisfied most of the Sioux's needs. Bancroft-Hunt lists a few of these as follows:

> Its sinews made fine cordage and bowstrings, and the hair was braided into ropes. Hammers, fleshing tools,

Sioux hunters pursue buffalo wearing animal skins to disguise their scent.

arrowshaft straighteners, dice and gambling sticks could be made from the bones and hooves; horns were boiled and made into ladles and bowls, or used as powder flasks; while skulls were important in ceremonies. A yellow paint could be obtained from the gallstones, and this was mixed with buffalo fat for use; tails made tipi ornaments, the paunch a water bucket, while ribs were lashed together as makeshift sledges and the tips of horns formed spinning tops in children's games.[7]

The buffalo provided all of the women's sewing needs—bone awls for punching holes through tough hides and sinew thread to sew them together. Sinew was also used as a fishing line, with a buffalo-bone hook.

Of primary importance to the Sioux was the meat. After a successful hunt, they would feast for days on fresh meat. The hump was considered tastiest, and the shoulder was often reserved for religious ceremonies. Other meat was cut into long strips and set out in the sun to dry. Some of this went into pemmican for the lean winter months. Successful hunts meant the difference between life and death for the Sioux. If unprepared for winter, the women had to feed their families boiled hide scrapings. There was no such thing as too much dried buffalo meat during a Great Plains winter.

The buffalo hides served as clothing, bedding, and shelter. Preparing these was hard work. The women staked the hide on flat ground and scraped off the excess fat and flesh with bone tools before allowing it to dry. Bancroft-Hunt describes the use of the unprocessed hide known as rawhide:

Some untanned skins made a flexible, lightweight, waterproof and virtually unbreakable rawhide which could be used for making anything that required semi-rigid strength, from the large rawhide envelopes, or parfleches, used for storage, to shields, rattles, drums and lacing thongs. Advantage was taken of the shrinkage that occurs in rawhide to bind stone heads to war clubs, and to make wood frame saddles: the wet hide was sewn into place, completely covering the frame, and as it dried it tightened about the joints, preventing them from loosening in use.[8]

Tepee hides were tanned, which involved scraping off the hair and treating the rawhide with buffalo fat and brains. Some of the tanned hides were further processed and smoked over the tepee fire to make them water-resistant. The smoked hides were used for clothing and containers such as parfleches and shield covers.

The drying and tanning of buffalo hides was a difficult and time-consuming task for Sioux women.

The Teton Sioux Calendar

The Sioux measured their months in "moons," labeling them by the seasonal changes naturally occurring between each full moon. Some of these changes had to do with weather, the Sioux's greatest friend or worst enemy. Others had to do with changes in the growing season and concerned the type of food to be had during that moon. In his book *Sioux Trail* John Upton Terrell presents the Teton Calendar as follows.

January—The Moon of Popping Trees (split with cold)
February—The Moon of Sore Eyes (snow blindness)
March—The Moon When the First Grain (plants) Come Up
April—The Moon of the Birth of (bison) Calves
May—The Moon of Strawberries
June—The Moon of Ripe Berries
July—The Moon of Chokecherries Ripening
August—The Moon of Ripe Plums
September—The Moon of Calves Growing Black (also, the Moon of Yellow Leaves)
October—The Moon of Falling Leaves
November—The Moon of Hairless Calves (fetuses found in slain bison cows)
December—The Moon of Frost in the Tepee

The Sioux Dog

Preparation of the buffalo kill was a time-consuming job and, after the custom of the Sioux, one done by the women. Their first concern was transporting the carcass back to camp, where they could work on it in comfort. To this end, they employed the dog. For as long as there have been Sioux, there have probably been Sioux dogs. It can be said that the dog taught the Lakota to walk, making possible their nomadic lifestyle. It was the dog that hauled back to camp the proceeds from the hunt, and the dog that was used to transport the tepee, possessions, and small children when the camp moved. This was accomplished with a travois. Only the largest dogs, generally males, were used as travois dogs. The strongest of these could haul seventy-five pounds per load.

Historian Royal B. Hassrick describes the Sioux dog's appearance as ranging "in color from blacks to grayish browns, with pointed faces and sharp ears, giving them a coyote-like appearance."[9] He also notes that the Sioux used their dogs for more than transport: "The Sioux had a variety of dogs; large animals about the size of a husky were preferred for working, while a smaller type was kept for eating."[10] At three months of age, puppies made a delicious meal for both family and ceremonial affairs. The Sioux dogs also performed guard duties and served as playmates for the younger children. Whether pulling the travois, serving as sentinel

The Sioux Tepee

Construction of the Sioux's home began with the procurement of roughly a dozen long sturdy poles, young sapling trees stripped of their branches and bark. Because the Upper Great Plains are in many places barren, the Sioux often obtained these poles from other tribes, trading hides for them. The three strongest of these poles formed the foundation of the Sioux tepee. These were raised upright and braced against one another at a point about five feet from their ends, creating a large triangle at their base. The remaining poles were then placed against these, their tops resting in the crotches created by the first three, their bases forming a large circle. Because the west winds are of the highest intensity, the back of the tepee was more angulated than the front, which always faced the east.

Once the poles had been placed, the outer covering was draped over them. This covering, made of buffalo hides, was tied in place about five feet from the top, with a flap left open for a door. Large stones were placed around the bottom edges of the te-pee, holding the hide down. These were left behind when the camp moved, and rings of these stones can still be seen in portions of the prairie. Some of the Sioux painted pictographs on the outside of their tepees, a series of pictures depicting the man of the house's exploits in battle and the hunt. Most, however, preferred to paint these histories on the inner lining, a hide cover about five feet wide that was lashed to the inside of the tepee for insulation. This inner cover served to keep the winds out, but when stuffed with dried prairie grass, it also helped the tepee retain its warmth.

The tepee was heated by a small fire in the center. The smoke rose up through the opening left at the top. Furnishings were simple. The Sioux fashioned backrests of willow and, seated on the floor around the fire, were able to lean back comfortably. The buffalo hides used for beds and bedding were placed in stacks around the tepee, serving as a sort of beanbag chair. When the wind howled in the winter, a family in a well-constructed tepee interior was warm and comfortable.

or friend, or just plain serving, the dog was important to the culture of the Sioux.

The arrival of the horse, however, lessened the dog's importance. If the dog can be credited with teaching the Sioux to walk, it was the horse that taught them to fly. Although the dog still held a place in the heart of the Sioux, it was the horse, what they called "the Sacred Dog," that held the place of honor.

Chapter 2

Dogs of War: The Horse and a Culture Based on War

Millions of years ago, eohippus, the ancestor of the horse, originated on the North American continent. Then, for reasons that remain one of paleontology's greatest mysteries, they became extinct on that continent. Fortunately for horse-lovers the world over, some of these tiny horse prototypes had managed to migrate to Europe and Asia, where they flourished. In the fifteenth century, the descendants of eohippus, now strong, tall, and very fast, made a triumphant return to North America via the ships of the Spanish explorers and colonists.

Many of the Native Americans were at first terrified when they saw the horse. Bearing on its back a strangely attired man, it looked like a savage, two-headed beast. It was not long, however, before they recognized their error and saw the advantages to be derived by possession of these wonderful animals. By the late sixteenth century, the Indians of the Southwest had become skilled horse thieves. Soon they had more than they could use and began trading the excess to other tribes. Passing from tribe to tribe, the horse worked its way to the Upper Great Plains.

Sometime between 1740 and 1770 the Sioux obtained the first of what they called "the Sacred Dog." Lakota tradition, according to author George E. Hyde, "states that the people obtained their first horses from the Arikaras"[11] in what is now central South Dakota. The Cheyenne, however, remember things differently, maintaining that "the first Sioux who came into their country arrived in little groups, all afoot. They came to beg for horses and each season returned in increasing numbers, until presently they were in sufficient strength to begin attacking other tribes."[12] Whatever its origins, the Sioux and the horse then initiated a partnership that has yet to be dissolved.

The Sacred Dog

The Indian horse was termed a *pony* because of its small size. A pony is generally a horse measuring under 14.2 hands—a hand equaling four inches—from the top of the withers to the ground. In the 1880s Samuel Sidney, a British horseman and author, described the typical Indian pony as follows:

> The pony used by the red Indians of America is scarcely fourteen hands in height, rather light than heavy in build, with good legs, straight shoulders (like all uncultivated horses?), short strong back, full barrel; he has no appearance of "blood" [good breeding], except sharp, nervous ears, and bright, intelligent eyes; but his endurance is incredible. He is never stalled, nor washed, nor dressed, nor blanketed, nor shod, nor fed. When not under saddle he is picketed or turned loose to shift for himself.

> In winter he is a terrible object—an animated skeleton. His pasture being buried beneath the snow, he would perish if the squaws did not cut branches of the cotton-wood trees for him to browse on. But when the spring brings out the tender grass he sheds his coat, scours [loses] his protuberant belly, and moves with head erect, ears and eyes full of intelligence. He will climb steep rocks like a mule, plunge down a perpendicular precipice like a buffalo; only the elk can more successfully cross swamps, and he will go at speed through sand-hills and ground

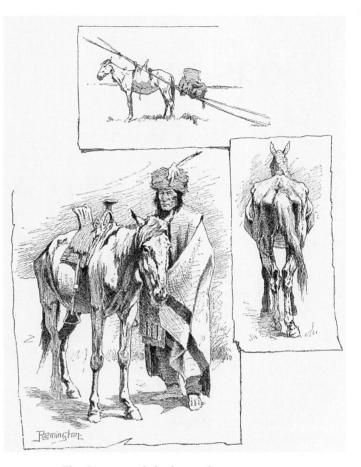

The Sioux used the horse for many purposes, including the hauling of supplies.

perforated with holes, where an American horse would fall in the first fifty yards of a gallop. The work he can do is astonishing.[13]

The Sioux quickly adapted to this tough pony, and it was not long before they gained a reputation as top horsemen. They could be harsh masters, though. Although some of the Sioux provided tiny shelters for their favorite mounts during the winter, feeding them small amounts of hay, bark, and branches, the majority of the horses braved the winters of the Upper Great Plains unprotected, pawing through the snow for food. Another rather brutal custom was to slice open the pony's nostrils to enhance its respiration, which was important when traveling long distances at any degree of speed. In 1770 fur trader Peter Pond wrote, "In order to have thare Horseis Long Winded [the Sioux] slit thair Noses up to the Grissel of thare head which Make them Breath Verey Freely."[14]

The Sioux's training methods ranged from gentle to harsh. Sioux boys began the early training by leading the ponies deep into a body of water and handling them there. This accustomed skittish young horses to being touched. According to Hassrick, that

Young-Man-Afraid-of-His-Horse

Many of the Sioux were named after the Sacred Dog. Some, like Crazy Horse, were given their name because they saw the horse in a vision. Others were given it for reasons that have become obscured through time. One of these, the great nineteenth-century diplomat Young-Man-Afraid-of-His-Horse, has become the subject of a great controversy.

George E. Hyde, author of *Red Cloud's Folks,* contends that this name was hereditary, passed from father to son, ergo the word *Young.* Noting that there was a Man-Afraid-of-His-Horse in the eighteenth century, Hyde states that it would not be unusual for a warrior to be afraid of his horse at that time. The eighteenth century marked the beginning of the Sioux's relationship with the horse. Horses were new to them and, there being rogues among horses just as there are rogues among men, it is not improbable that even the greatest of warriors would exercise extreme caution around a nasty horse. Hyde asks his readers to also consider the typical Sioux's well-developed sense of humor. It is possible that the first Man-Afraid-of-His-Horse was called this name in jest, and it stuck. Hyde's argument is compelling.

However, many other experts disagree. They maintain that the answer to this derogatory name lies not in the caution exercised by a warrior around a mean horse, but in the white man's translation of the difficult Siouan language. In *The Indian and His Horse,* Frank Gilbert Roe proclaims that "the misinterpretation of [this name] has furnished a subject for the measureless laughter of many fools. The true interpretation is, of course, 'Young Man (i.e., one whom years could not enfeeble, or eternal youth) whose very horses bring terror to his enemies!'"

Ideally, colts were not trained until they were three years old. Younger colts, it was believed, could be broken more easily, but older colts proved stronger and better disciplined. Boys, however, often trained yearlings, and oddly enough, such young animals were considered to become especially long-winded and good runners.[15]

The final training process could be brutal, however, involving several men wearing the horse down over a period of several hours.

Horse Training, Sioux Style

In his book *The Sioux: Life and Customs of a Warrior Society,* author Royal B. Hassrick describes the training of a young horse by the Sioux.

"A horse to be broken was first choked down with a noose about his neck while one man sat on its head. When the horse was well secured around the neck by two or three men at the end of a long rope, the man on his head jumped off, being careful to avoid the horse's kicking feet. Immediately the horse would spring up, and the men held to the rope allowing the animal to fight. As the horse battled the rope, the men gradually led him to the camp circle. Here the men wound the rope several times around the horse's legs and jerking suddenly, threw it to the ground. Quickly one of the men jumped on him as the others tied his front feet together and then secured these to the horse's left hind leg. When the horse was freed to rise, it was thrown by its hobble again and again. This ordeal lasted for whatever time it took to exhaust the animal.

When the horse was finally so tired that it lay upon the ground, too weak to struggle, the men thumped him lightly over his body and especially over his neck and ears and back. After tapping him thoroughly, they threw a robe over the animal's back. The horse generally bucked and jumped trying to throw off the robe, but being hobbled, fell again and again in its struggle. When the horse could no longer muster strength enough to throw off the robe, one of the men approached and gently jumped upon his back. Then the rider carefully placed a halter over his mouth. When it became evident that the animal was adjusted to the halter and rider, the others again tapped and patted and smoothed the horse's body. Then, with caution, the hobbling ropes were released, and the horse trotted off bearing his rider. To accomplish this pacification might take all day; some especially mean horses required two days to train. But in any case, the Sioux's method was effective enough to gain for them some of the world's best-trained, fastest, and most enduring horses."

Although harsh, tying down and working a horse to exhaustion was the Sioux method of breaking horses.

The Influence of the Horse

The horse was hugely responsible for the evolution of the Lakota into mighty Plains warriors. Prior to the horse, buffalo hunts had been difficult to control. The pound had no shutoff valve to prevent an entire herd from plummeting over a cliff, nor did it allow the Sioux to select which buffalo would be involved. The Sioux often killed more buffalo than needed, including less desirable old bulls. Mounted on a horse, the Sioux were able to hunt selectively. Guiding his horse with his knees, a hunter approached a herd of buffalo at high speeds, easing his mount alongside the preferred cows and young bulls and, after discharging his arrow, diving quickly away before the beast tumbled to the ground. The Sioux could now control the quantity and quality of buffalo killed.

The horse's influence went beyond improved hunting conditions. "Possession of the animals brought great advantages to the Plains nomads," writes Alvin M. Josephy Jr., noting that

the substitution of horses for dogs meant that loads lashed to travois poles could become bigger; larger supplies of dried meat could be packed from the sites of kills for use at later times; and longer lodge poles could be dragged, making possible the construction of taller and roomier tipis. Hunters gained greater mobility and freedom of movement, and with the ability to roam over larger distances for longer periods of time, their chances for successful hunts increased.[16]

Because the travois could carry more, the elderly and the ill could be transported when moving camps. The Sioux's bent for generosity was also easily satisfied with the horse. Even the poor owned at least one horse.

Not all of the horse's influence was positive. With it came a widening of class structure that weakened the Sioux's strong sense of community. The horse was used for trade, as "money" to buy necessities and luxuries, so the family with the most horses was able to buy the nicest things. This family was also able to transport the most goods, so it could accumulate the most possessions. And the horse provided the means for its owner to acquire more horses through theft. The Sioux deemed generosity the highest of all virtues, but their social system was centered on individual status and prestige. As a result,

The horse allowed the Sioux to transport more supplies and people during their migrations.

Their skill with the horse contributed to the Sioux's reputation as dangerous warriors.

slight economic gaps had always existed between the families led by great hunter-warriors and those led by men possessing less skill. However, the horse widened these gaps to chasms. The family with a hundred horses was considerably wealthier than one with only a few, spawning envy and resentment.

Theorists also argue that the acquisition of the horse contributed to the decimation of the buffalo herds, charging that the Indians killed more buffalo simply because they now could. Some maintain that the boost the horse provided to their economy promoted wastefulness, arguing that they were rocketed from a life of want to one of plenty and became complacent as a result. It has also been suggested that the ability

to travel longer distances generated cultural instability because of the rapidity of environmental change and the increased contact with other cultures. However, even the nay-saying theorists cannot ignore the positive influence of the horse when it came to that which the Sioux held most dear: the waging of war.

The horse was the Sioux dream machine, providing its warriors with the means of obtaining prestige in battle. They could now exercise a lightning-fast raid or mount a full-scale offensive. Sioux warriors could sweep down on an enemy camp, stealing horses and other property, and be well away before the camp inhabitants had so much as pulled on their breechcloths. They could approach an enemy war party at speeds in excess of forty miles per hour even as they notched arrows to their bowstrings. Sioux warriors could now wage efficient war, expert war, beautifully choreographed war. Ultimately, that was the foundation of the Sioux culture: war.

A Culture Based on War

Some psychologists maintain that an individual's actions are based on three things: genetic inheritance, the situation, and learned behavior. The same might apply when attempting to understand the Sioux's love of war. They certainly possessed the genetic inheritance. Although intertribal marriages were not forbidden, the Sioux generally married tribal members who were descended from like ancestors, ancestors to whom war had been a way of life. The offspring produced from these marriages possessed a genetic heritage tracing back from time immemorial to great warrior after great warrior.

The situation was one of conflict. Many of the tribes of the era were equally warlike. The Sioux had a standing enmity with the Crow and the Pawnee and did not require any excuse to wage war against them. They also fought in retaliation for past offenses and to defend themselves and their property. Most importantly, they fought to protect their territory. The Sioux were one of several nations denoted "buffalo Indians," meaning they depended on the buffalo for their livelihood. They had favorite hunting sites to which they returned year after year. Should another tribe encroach on this territory before them, killing the buffalo and running them off, the winter ahead would be lean. Therefore, the Sioux waged war out of necessity.

The reason for the Sioux's absolute enjoyment of war, however, lies in learned behavior. There was no greater honor to be achieved than that of having acquitted oneself well in battle. From the moment a young Sioux boy could walk and talk, he was taught this behavior. From the first time he listened to returning warriors boast of their success in battle, he learned that the route to prestige lay in his own eventual successes as a warrior. Much as a contemporary youth might dream of one

day excelling at a career in law or medicine, the Sioux boy dreamed of excelling in battle.

He also dreamed of excelling in the actions that spawned battles. Historian Robert West Howard reports that "stealing the horses of a rival tribe became a feat that won social prestige. The Sioux, especially, relished horse-thievery as a brave sport. . . . One of the proudest achievements a young warrior could dream about was to 'get right into the village circle and steal the favorite horse of some important warrior.'"[17] To do so was an opportunity to demonstrate the courage necessary for status. A young man might also win status through "success in hunting, power through a vision, membership in a society, presentation of ceremonies, and exhibition of generosity."[18] The preferred choice, however, was to win fame as a warrior.

The Art of War

As much as the Sioux relished a good battle, the process behind the decision to engage in war was methodical, especially when the motive for the fight was retaliation. Hyde outlines the procedure as follows:

The customs that were observed on these occasions were fixed. . . . The expedition did not set out as soon as news was received that a party of their warriors had met disaster; the people waited "one winter" and during that time the relatives of the dead men took the war pipe to neighboring camps where they publicly

Scalping

The Sioux engaged in the practice of scalping. Many experts believe the French originated this custom among the Native Americans when they paid Indians a bounty on scalps in the French and Indian War. However, in his book *The Colorful Story of the American West,* Sioux expert Royal B. Hassrick argues that scalping originated because of the Indian belief that hair was "akin to the spirit and with life everlasting." Therefore, when a man was killed in battle and circumstances were such that his comrades could not retrieve his body, they replaced his spirit with the scalp of a slain enemy. Thus began the practice of scalping.

When Sioux warriors returned to camp after a battle in which men had been lost, a scalp dance was held. John Upton Terrell, author of *Sioux Trail,* reports that scalps were not deemed trophies.

"[Scalps] were kept only until a scalp dance had been held to celebrate a victory or a successful raid. It was customary for Sioux warriors to give scalps to their women folk, who would sew them to small willow hoops which they tied to long poles. After drying them properly in the sun, the women would wave the scalp poles proudly during the scalp dance. Sometimes bits of enemy hairs were saved to fasten onto war shirts or to braid into a person's own locks."

Hassrick contends that enemy scalps were given only to the female relatives of the fallen man, such as a mother or a sister. According to him, these scalps were presented with a formal statement: "Here is your son. Now his spirit may join his body. Now he will be permitted to enter the 'Land of many Lodges.' Dance with this and rejoice for your son is now one."

The scalps of Native Americans were the most desirable, but the scalp of a white man would suffice when these were not available.

Scalping was seen as a way to bring back the spirit of a slain warrior.

mourned their dead and pleaded with the people to help them. In each camp the leading men held councils and decided whether their chiefs should accept the pipe or reject it. The pipe was nearly always accepted, and when it had been smoked by the chiefs the camp was pledged to take part in the forthcoming expedition.[19]

A time was scheduled, with early winter and summer preferred. Generally, within a year of offense having been given, the Sioux enacted a retaliatory war.

The Sioux utilized set tactics when conducting a major offensive. Much as they did during major buffalo hunts, the Sioux often moved entire camps when tracking human prey. According to Hyde,

> The camps assembled and moved as secretly and swiftly as they could into the enemy's country, with scouts out ahead to look for hostile camps. Having arrived near one of these camps, a halt was made on some stream; here the camps with the women, children, and old men were left, while the warriors . . . attempted to surprise the enemy camp at dawn.[20]

The Sioux also enjoyed great success with the decoy method of fighting. With this technique, a few Sioux warriors would appear within visual range of a large enemy party. Seeing this small number of mounted Sioux and smelling an easy victory, the enemy would engage in immediate pursuit. Urging their ponies on to greater speed, the Sioux warriors led the enemy to a predetermined location where the rest of their party waited in silence, arrows notched. Use of the decoy method enabled the Sioux to select the best location for a pitched battle.

Weapons

Some of the early fighting was done with clubs, shields, and even, in the case of one Yanktonai chief, a suit of rawhide body armor. When the Sioux obtained horses, much of this changed. No one wore body armor; it was too uncomfortable when mounted. Although decorated shields were still coveted, most remained behind in their specially designed covers when the warriors rode into battle. The war club, a decorated hammerlike tool, was still used to dispatch the wounded enemies after battle, sparing the Sioux the use of valuable arrows and ammunition.

Another important weapon was the lance, a long spearlike weapon carried by members of special clubs, or fraternities. Each fraternity had a distinctive design for its lances, so it was easy to tell to which club a warrior belonged. During battle, these fraternity members made good use of their lances. They were a lethal weapon when driven with force through the enemy's chest. They could be used to count coup, striking the enemy, though some preferred to use their bare hand or a coup stick. Some fraternity members thrust their lances into the ground during a battle, dismounting and standing beside them while they fought. In these cases, the warrior could not leave the scene of the battle unless another member of his fraternity removed the lance from the ground.

The Sioux's favorite weapon was the bow and arrow. Each warrior prepared the feathering on his arrows in a unique manner. After a battle or a hunt, it was therefore easy to determine who was responsible for which kill. This was especially important after a hunt, when the division of the carcasses was made. Widows and the wives of lesser warriors could claim a quarter of a carcass by tying its tail, but the bulk of the carcass went to the man whose arrow had brought it down. The identification of kills was also important after a battle. The Sioux liked to boast of their prowess as warriors, and it was a matter of reputation to be able to prove responsibility for many dead enemies.

The lightweight bow and arrow was in some ways superior to the cumbersome muzzle-loading rifles used by the early white men. Author Walter Prescott Webb states that "the loading [of these weapons] was a meticulous and time-consuming task. The powder had to be measured and poured, the ball had to be rammed down the barrel with a long rod, the tube must be 'primed,' and the cap or flint had to be adjusted."[21] By the time a spent muzzle-loading rifle was again ready to fire, a well-mounted Sioux could have raced his horse a quarter of a mile while firing close to two dozen arrows. Although these rifles were superior in terms of destruction, the bow and arrow could not be beat for rapidity of firing.

Decorated with a variety of multicolored feathers and skins, the Sioux used numerous tools and weapons for hunting and waging war.

Counting Coup

No individual action performed during a battle was more important to the up-and-coming Sioux warrior than that of counting coup. *Coup* is a French word meaning "blow"; to "count coup" meant to strike a blow against the enemy. This blow could be struck with a lance, a special coup stick, or one's bare hand, with the latter being the most prestigious of all. If done while the enemy was still alive, it was that much the better.

There were rigid regulations regarding the amount of prestige to be achieved. The first warrior to count coup on an enemy was accorded four status "points," the second three points. Third and fourth won two and one points, respectively, and all blows after that earned nothing. Killing an enemy was not considered as prestigious as counting coup because it took tremendous courage to touch an enemy in the heat of battle. A warrior may have a dozen enemies converging on him from all sides, but he was nonetheless determined to count coup on the fallen, the riderless, or in some cases, even on the well mounted and armed.

Amos Bad Heart Bull, an Oglala born in 1869, recorded his knowledge of Oglala history in a series of over four hundred stirring pictographs, which can be seen in Helen H. Blish's *A Pictographic History of the Oglala Sioux*. Many of these pictographs portray battles between the Sioux and their favorite enemy, the Crow. One in particular demonstrates the dark side of counting coup. A lone Sioux warrior stands between the two mounted forces. He has ridden forward to count coup on a dismounted Crow. Unfortunately, he will not live to recount the exploit. He is shot as he races back to join his own forces.

In the text accompanying the pictograph, Blish writes, "Especially great was the honor if this were done to a live enemy; consequently, warriors not infrequently risked their lives, with apparent foolhardiness and often with fatal results."

The invention of breechloaders, first used in the United States during its Civil War, changed that. Reloading required only that the bullet chamber be opened, a bullet rammed in, and the chamber snapped shut. And it was not long before the repeating rifle, one with multishot capacity, was invented. Had ammunition been readily available, these repeating rifles would have replaced the bow and arrow. However, the whites were in no hurry to supply the fierce Sioux with ammunition, and the Sioux did not know how to make their own. When ammunition was scarce, the Sioux returned to their old standby, the bow and arrow.

There is a seeming contradiction to be seen when studying the Sioux's approach to war. The decision to engage in a major battle was the result of a somber, well-considered process determined by a council of elders. Yet the battle itself was feverish, fought by warriors with adrenaline so high that they wanted nothing more than the honor of dying. It would almost seem like two tribes were involved: the one careful, the other careless. The reason for this apparent contradiction lies in the Sioux's social and political organization, in the structure that bound the individual to the society.

Chapter 3

Social and Political Organization: The Individual, the Band, the Tribe

Although the Sioux frequently acted as individuals and were free to determine their own path at any given time, it was their way to behave as part of a whole. An ideal analogy for this can be found in a colony of killer bees. The queen, workers, and drones buzz pleasantly as they leisurely perform their respective tasks. However, when attacked by a bear the buzz becomes angry as the bees swarm, diving in to sting the intruder. Each bee is only a nuisance by itself but, working in concert with the others, lethal to the bear. So operated the Sioux at the level of the individual, always part of the hive, always first and foremost a Sioux, yet acting as such only when the need arose. Each Sioux performed a predetermined role based on gender and age. When not under attack or hunting, when not partaking in religious or political ceremonies, the individual concentrated on individual autonomy.

The Individual

For the men, this meant assuming the role of warrior and hunter as well as that of

politician and/or policeman, which were simple but dangerous tasks. The elderly within a family group took on the role of adviser and helper. The elderly women, though often lacking the physical strength to process meat or hides, helped care for the children. They also turned their hand to sewing, cooking, and cleaning, and it is to be supposed that the mothers-in-law were free with advice to their daughters-in-law regarding these chores. The elderly men played a major role in the government, serving as calm, collected advisers to the relatively hotter heads of the young men.

The role of the children was of equal importance. Even the youngest helped pick berries and carry water to the lodge. At an early age, the girls began helping their mothers with the daily chores. By the age of twelve they were talented seamstresses and were highly skilled in the art of beadwork and quill decoration, preparing exquisitely decorated moccasins for the entire family. The boys, armed with miniature bows and arrows, hunted small game to supplement the family food supplies. Often they brought home the eggs, turtles, fish, and other delicacies that provided the family with a break from their buffalo-meat diets.

The women did the bulk of the heavy work. Not only did they perform the tasks that most cultures assign to women—cooking, sewing, cleaning, and child care—but they also were responsible for the chores related to the moving of the camp and the preparation of the kill. When the camp moved, it was the women who

Sioux warriors in full ceremonial dress prepare to engage in a celebration of their accomplishments.

dismantled the tepees, set up the travois, packed the goods, and handled the dogs and horses. Upon arrival at the new campsite, it was the women who erected the tepees. After a hunt, the women were responsible for preparing both meat and hides and for sewing new tepee covers when the old ones rotted from moisture.

This time invested in dismantling, erecting, and making tepee covers was not without its rewards. In the Sioux society, the women owned their own homes. "In fact," maintains historian Norman Bancroft-Hunt, "men had little say in matters concerning the home: the women owned the tipi, house-willow rods, as well as the kettle and tripod used in cooking; the parfleche containers of dried meat were hers, as was any meat her husband secured while hunting."[22] Although the women worked constantly at exhausting labor, they took pride in the work done.

From Family to Band

The next level of Sioux social organization was the family, a collection of relatives residing together. As noted by Bancroft-Hunt,

The strongest commonly held obligation was to one's relatives, and family ties tend to emphasize the integrated nature of Plains social life. A close family, always camping together and occupying

Needlework

The Sioux ceremonial attire was beautifully hand decorated, and the pieces in museums today are still admired as some of the finest needlework to arise from any culture, past or present. The Sioux women performed exquisite masterpieces on leather or rawhide. White prairie clay was often worked into the leather first, making it a creamy white color. Then porcupine quills were dyed and worked into the leather, generally in geometric designs. Elk teeth and shells were occasionally interspersed as well. Wedding dresses, moccasins, shirts, parfleches, shield covers—anything of ceremonial and personal significance were decorated in this fashion.

Working with porcupine quills was difficult. A particularly elaborate article of clothing might require hundreds of these quills, each attached individually. One highly decorated item might represent days, even weeks, of work. The arrival of the fur traders relieved some of this toil. They brought with them colored beads, shiny buttons, tiny mirrors, and brightly colored ribbons and cloth, all of which to a certain extent supplanted quills and teeth. They also brought advanced sewing tools, which made the job that much easier. Many still preferred the old ways, however, and porcupine quills remained a mainstay into the twentieth century.

several tipis, might include grandparents and great-grandparents, unmarried brothers and sisters, parents and children; possibly totalling thirty or more individuals.[23]

This collection of relatives, known as an extended family, was of special benefit to the Sioux children. Unlike the nuclear family, which consists of parents and their children, it was not uncommon for a Sioux child to emerge from his or her tepee in the morning to the greetings of countless relatives. This provided the children with a sense of security and continuity. Additionally, because aunts and uncles served as secondary parents to their nieces and nephews, there was no such thing as an orphan.

The extended family was the seed from which a band often sprouted. There were a number of reasons why the leader of a family, its "headman," may choose to strike out on his own. Maybe his own band had grown beyond a manageable size, or perhaps he disagreed with the policies of the band council. Whatever the reason, he packed up his family and moved. Now if this man was a good hunter and a brave warrior who actively practiced the four Sioux virtues of courage, fortitude, generosity, and wisdom, other families were likely to follow. According to Royal B. Hassrick, "The reputation of a headman attracted not only his immediate family but also distant relatives and friends, who might abandon a less capable leader to place their trust in him."[24]

Among the Sioux, several members of an extended family often set up camp together.

And so a new band was formed. Much as the Sioux family is a collection of relatives, a large band is a collection of families. Bancroft-Hunt defines a band, what some experts call a "camp," as follows:

The band was a social entity: a definite group consisting of a series of families united both politically and economically under the leadership of a band-chief and council and averaging about three hundred members, although there was considerable variation on this. Since families were usually too small to offer adequate

protection and tribes too large to operate economically for extended periods under the conditions of Plains environments, the band was the basic unit to which a person belonged.[25]

The size of a band was determined by the availability of resources. It did not take long for three hundred Sioux and their horses to deplete the natural resources in any given area. Any more than three hundred would compel the camp into constant moves in search of forage, game, and fresh water.

When the band was small, composed of only a few dozen members, its political organization was simple. Although all looked to the headman for leadership, the elders determined policy. However, once the band grew beyond the capabilities of a headman and a handful of elders, the government flowered into a highly complex system under the guidance of volunteers. At that time, two types of societies, or clublike fraternities, were formed: police and civil. The police fraternities were responsible for law enforcement and were similar to modern police forces. The civil societies had multiple purposes, including improving morale and determining band policy. It was a matter of prestige to be a member of these fraternities, and most Sioux men were anxious to join.

☀

The Concept of Chief

What exactly was a Sioux chief? *Chief* is not a Sioux word, nor is it a Sioux concept. Early representatives of the fledgling United States of America found that their dealings with the Native American tribes were easier when they thought of them as possessing governments similar to their own. Thus, they labeled tribe leaders "chiefs."

However, in the government actually practiced by the Sioux, the term *chief* causes confusion. Although the Sioux system of government can be, for ease of comprehension, likened to that of the U.S. government, with its president/chief and congress/executive council, it was actually dissimilar in many aspects. The primary difference lay in the power of the so-called chief. If he advocated an unpopular policy, the nomadic Sioux people merely packed up their families and left, joining a band with a leader more to their liking.

Headman is the correct term for a chief, but the band chief was much, much more than a headman. Crazy Horse, for example, was a headman, a Shirt Wearer, a powerful member of the executive council,

the recipient of many visions, and was highly popular with his Oglala people and greatly respected as a warrior. Sitting Bull was a headman, a member of the Strong Heart fraternity, a holy man possessing extraordinary visionary powers, and, like Crazy Horse, was highly popular and greatly respected by his Hunkpapa tribe.

James R. Walker, agency physician on the Oglala Pine Ridge Reservation from 1896 to 1914, describes the route from family headman to band chief as being an evolutionary process. A family headman became a band chief when his small group achieved the size of a band. If there was more than one headman in the band, the one possessing the most status became band chief. When two bands merged, the procedure was similar, with the most powerful of the two band chiefs becoming chief of the combined forces. Because power and policy are in a constant state of flux, chief was a fluid concept to the Sioux. For example, one day Red Cloud was "chief" of the Oglala; by the next day it was Crazy Horse.

Akicitas: Police Societies

The Sioux police societies were called *akicitas*. There were a number of these, including the Kit Foxes, Plain Lance Owners, Badgers, Strong Hearts, Crow Owners, and White-Marked Ones. Each *akicita* practiced its own ceremonies and utilized

its own identifying lances and attire, but their purpose was the same: to prevent disruptive behavior. Only one group was in power, however, at any given time. The band executive council chose which fraternity would be responsible for the policing of any hunt, war, or move. The police society chosen took its task seriously.

Each *akicita* was organized similarly, with minor variations from society to society. Usually each had twelve officers, generally two each of pipe bearers, drummers, rattlers, and whippers, and four lance owners. The role of the pipe bearers was to counsel, mediate, and provide the voice of reason. The drummers and rattlers played integral roles in fraternity ceremonies. The whippers handled discipline of both *akicita* members and band individuals. The role of lance owners could be highly dangerous. As has been noted, some of them fought beside their lances in battle. According to Hassrick, "So strict were the requirements of officership that young men were frequently reluctant to accept the honor, knowing that to fulfill the obligations successfully was tantamount to death."[26]

Requirements for membership in an *akicita* were stringent, and it says a great deal about the average Sioux male that half of the eligible population belonged to one of these societies. Hassrick lists the requirements as follows:

> To be invited into the Akicita societies, a boy must usually have been on at least one war party, even if in no greater capacity than that of water

Displaying their weapons and other ceremonial items, a band of Sioux warriors pose for this 1898 picture.

boy. He would be considered an even more desirable candidate if he were the member of an outstanding family and had killed an enemy or "gone on the hill" to seek a vision. Youths of low status who had not sought a vision might not be invited until their middle twenties. Individuals could make up for the absence of supernatural power or for a modest family background by an exemplary war record. But a man who had committed murder or adultery, or who had amassed wealth by not giving feasts, was not eligible for membership. Neither would a poor hunter or an inept warrior be asked to join.[27]

Civil Societies

The civil societies varied in purpose. The White-Horse Owners society appears to have been devoted to improving morale. As their title suggests, these men rode only white horses because the color symbolized purity. White also served as an ideal canvas for the symbolic paintings these warriors used to depict past successes in battle, such as a handprint representing coup counted and a hoofprint

Akicita Enforcement

The *akicitas* took their duties as policemen, judges, and executioners very seriously. As policemen, they determined that an infraction had been committed. As judges, they handed down sentence on the offender, determining his punishment. And as executioners, they exacted the punishment. In his book *Plains Indians: Dog Soldiers, Bear Men, and Buffalo Women,* Thomas E. Mails outlines the law enforcement procedure.

"If the chiefs decided to move the camp on the following day, the Police were so informed, and when morning came, they would ride about the camp and see that all made ready to take the trail . . . if one should refuse (without acceptable reason) to obey the command, the Police would cut his tipi to pieces and might kill a horse or two. If the man being punished gave vent to anger, his life might be forfeited on the spot."

Regarding hunting infractions, Mails has this to say:

"Any man who began to hunt before the proper ceremonies were completed or before the signal was given to begin was severely beaten by the Police, sometimes to insensibility. His horse might be killed, his clothing cut to pieces and his weapons broken, as well. After all, any premature action on the part of a hunter showed selfishness and might well stampede the herd. Thus if someone evidenced even the slightest resentment when he was disciplined, he was likely to be killed. The same treatment was accorded a man who stole away from a band while it was on the march and killed a lone buffalo, even if he hadn't alarmed the herd."

representing horses stolen. Members of the White-Horse Owners often held a parade before a major hunt or battle, and the sight of these warriors on their painted white horses heated the blood of young and old alike.

The most important civil society was the Naca Ominicias, or the Big Bellies, so labeled because of the protuberant bellies possessed by its members. Without exception, membership in this society was restricted to older men of great renown. Hassrick reports that "members of this group were a kind of congress of patriarchs, including former headmen, famous retired hunters and warriors, and distinguished shamans, definitely past their prime and endowed with the pompous proportions of middle age."[28] These older men were responsible for determining policy regarding hunting, camp movements, and proposed wars. Members of the band executive council were drawn from this society, and it was the Naca Ominicias who appointed tribal administrators and executives, generally selecting them from its own membership.

One example of a Naca appointment is the "Shirt Wearers." The Shirt Wearers were spokesmen for the executive council, presenting Naca decisions to the people. They also mediated quarrels and often represented their bands at negotiations with other nations. The Shirt Wearers were so named because of the war shirts they were presented upon selection. These shirts were painted in a variety of colors, such as red, yellow, or black, with the colors representing aspects of Mother Earth, whom the wearers were sworn to protect. Each shirt was fringed with hair, reminding the wearer of the people for whom he was responsible. The Shirt Wearers carried into battle the ceremonial weapons of shield, lance, and headdress, hanging the shield on the rear of their saddle, the headdress on the horn, and holding their lances high.

Another example of a Naca appointment is the Pipe Owners, or *Wakincuzas,* who were responsible for directing camp movements, as Hassrick outlines:

The particular responsibility of the Wakincuzas centered in the organization of all camp moves, including the appointment of the Akicitas or police. They assigned camping locations to the bands and to the individual families. They determined the time and location of the periodic halts and rests. It was also their responsibility to give the order for large tribal hunts and surrounds. As officers of the march, the Wakincuzas walked far in advance of the main body of tribesmen. They directed all of the activities of the Akicitas, who as policemen and soldiers flanked the motley procession, kept it in order, and guarded against possible enemy attack.[29]

Seven Council Fires: Original and Lakotan

A band was nothing more than a manageable subdivision of a tribe. Although the Sioux took pride in their bands, often

43

naming them after an animal or a famous headman, they took even more pride in their status as tribal members. And a tribe was nothing more than a subdivision of the nation. Above all, the Sioux thought of themselves as members of the Seven Council Fires Nation. National meetings of the original Seven Council Fires did not occur during the nineteenth century, but when these seven woodland allies met for a great seventeenth-century council, it was customary to seat the tribal representatives according to the status of their tribe. In the early 1600s, the best seat went to the Dakota Mdewakanton representatives. However, the Lakota were then maturing into an extraordinarily powerful tribe. At the end of the seventeenth century, the Lakota took precedence at any Seven Council Fires meetings.

By the beginning of the eighteenth century the Lakota had split into their own Seven Council Fires. These seven tribes were the Oglala, the Brule, the Miniconjou, and four tribes referred to as "Saones" by the Lewis and Clark expedition: the Hunkpapa, the Sans Arcs (Without Bows), the Two Kettles, and the Blackfoot Sioux. At a Lakota council, the Oglala tribe was granted primary status. Had the white invasion occurred a half-century later, it is probable that the whites would have considered the Lakota a separate nation, exclusive of the old Seven Council Fires, or Sioux. This is important when attempting to understand the Sioux because comprehension of the Sioux requires placing an emphasis on the Lakota.

Description of a Yanktonai Chief

One of the duties of office was to dress in a manner appropriate to both the situation and one's position. In the case of the societies, dress was determined by code. A headman, however, was not so restricted. Of primary importance, however, was that he make as striking an impression as possible, particularly when dealing with foreigners. In his book *Sioux Trail,* John Upton Terrell quotes a description of a Nakota, or Yanktonai, headman encountered by the American explorer, Major Stephen H. Long.

"Long described one Yanktonai chieftain as wearing 'a splendid cloak of buffalo skins, dressed so as to be a fine white color, which was decorated with tufts of owl feathers and other of various hues. His necklace was formed of about 60 claws of the grizzly bear, and his leggings, jacket, and moccasins were of white skins profusely decorated with human hair, the moccasins being variegated with plumage from several birds. In his hair, secured by a strip of red cloth, he wore 9 sticks neatly cut and smoothed and painted with vermillion, which designated the number of gunshot wounds he had received. His hair was plaited in two tresses, which hung forward; his face was painted with vermillion, and in his hand he carried a large fan of turkey feathers.'"

Much has been written about the Lakota, particularly the Oglala tribe. Unfortunately, there is considerably less information about the seminomadic Dakota and Nakota. This may be because they were the first to capitulate to the whites, and many of their ways were lost as a result. More likely, they were simply overshadowed by the colorful Lakota nomads. Whatever the cause, much of the information available on the Sioux references the Lakota. It can nevertheless be assumed that, having shared the same origins, the Dakota, Lakota, and Nakota shared many of the same customs and religious beliefs. For it is from the Sioux customs and religious beliefs that a non-Sioux can best comprehend the actions of the people of the Sioux Nation.

The foregoing system of social and political organization, for example, was highly complex and, as such, confusing to the non-Sioux. Unfamiliar with the political practices of the people, representatives of the U.S. government frequently made the error of assuming that the Sioux government was structured similar to their own. As Lakota author Vine Deloria Jr. writes, "The early colonists, accustomed to life under benevolent despots, projected their understanding of the European political structure onto the Indian tribe in trying to explain its political and social structure."[30] Crediting band executives with a power beyond that delegated was one such error. The U.S. government often negotiated agreements only to later learn that one Sioux warrior, no matter how powerful, no matter how prestigious, could not decide the fate of his people.

The same error was made with Sioux social practices. The ways of the Sioux were not the ways of the U.S. government or those of its citizens. These U.S. citizens, generally of European descent, did not understand the Sioux. Because humans tend to fear that which they do not understand and to hate that which they fear, these citizens came to fear and hate the Sioux. Had they taken the time to look at the customs and religious beliefs of the people, perhaps many of the unhappy events that occurred in the latter part of the nineteenth century could have been avoided.

Chapter 4

Customs and Religion: In Worship of Wakan Tanka

The Sioux were an ethnocentric people. This means that they believed their culture was the only correct culture. Although they established friendships with a few other tribes, they believed that all other cultures were inferior. This ethnocentricity was reflected in their relationships with other nations. The Sioux morality applied only to the Sioux, not to others, contributing to a curious double standard. Behavior that was acceptable for, and even required of, the Sioux did not apply to non-Sioux tribes.

Their attitude toward homicide provides an excellent example of this double standard. When a Sioux murdered another Sioux, it was not considered an offense against society, and the *akicitas* did not become involved. The relatives of the deceased could retaliate, but if the murderer was strong, possessing great status, he often went free. But woe to the non-Sioux who foolishly took the life of one of the people. In that case, he brought down upon himself the wrath of an entire nation.

Marriage customs provide yet another example. If a Sioux man married a non-Sioux captive, she was granted none of the courtesy given a Sioux woman. Although, according to historian James R. Walker, "it was esteemed an honor to have a wife who was captured from an alien people, especially if the people were hereditary enemies,"[31] a captured wife was already the property of her captor, so there was no need for ceremony. She simply became both property and wife. A Sioux woman, on the other hand, enjoyed an elaborate courtship ritual.

Marriage Customs

To propose to a Sioux woman, a man painted his face, dressed in his finest clothes, and flung about his shoulders the courting robe. He paced back and forth before her tepee until she came to the door. Drawing nearer, the warrior grabbed her. She pretended to struggle, but only briefly. Covering himself and the woman with the robe, the man spoke to her. The woman's guardians invited the two inside, where they seated themselves. If the woman did not want the man, she turned her back on him. If she welcomed marriage, she smiled and brought him a drink of water, telling him to visit again. When he returned she offered him food she had prepared, and she presented him with a pair of moccasins she had made. The two parties were now engaged.

During the engagement, the woman wore her braids down her back, and the man courted her, playing a flute outside her tepee in the evenings. Sometimes her friends burned cottonwood twigs to eliminate future marital strife. A price was then set for the young woman. A man generally agreed to pay her guardians six buffalo skins or two horses, though an especially hardworking and sweet-tempered woman

Divorce

Divorce was not uncommon among the Sioux, possibly because it was an easy procedure. If a Sioux man chose to divorce his wife, all he needed to do was to announce it publicly. If he was a member of one of the police societies, he announced it during one of the ceremonies, beating on a drum and telling all present that he no longer wanted his wife. He could then sell her, give her away, or abandon her. A woman divorced her husband by asking him to leave. If he did not leave, she could enlist the support of her relatives to expel him.

Sioux custom mandated that there be sufficient cause for a divorce. Men could divorce a wife who was argumentative, lazy, selfish, or unfaithful. Infidelity by a woman was considered the most heinous of marital offenses. If divorce was not chosen, a man might punish his wife for a first offense by cutting off one of her braids. A second offense might result in him disfiguring her by cutting off her nose

or one of her ears. If the behavior continued, he was within his rights to kill her. Women could divorce a husband who was abusive or unfaithful. If a woman did not want a divorce from an unfaithful husband, she could publicly beat him. He endured the clubbing because to run would expose him to the ridicule of the female population. Most Sioux, however, chose to divorce an unfaithful spouse.

Children of a broken home did not suffer unduly. Children under the age of five or six stayed with their mother. If the mother remarried, these children became the offspring of her new husband. The older children were allowed to remain with their parent of choice. However, the Sioux practice of an extended family precluded the type of lengthy separation from either parent endured by members of the nuclear family. The children still saw each parent on a daily basis, no matter which parent they chose.

could command much more. Once the price was paid, a great feast was given by the woman's guardians. After the feast the woman led the man to her tepee, where she put moccasins on his feet and took her place at the right side of the fire. The couple was now married, and the woman could wear her braids in the front.

One exception to the marriage ritual concerned abductions. Abductions were caused by the Sioux's practice of polygamy, of taking more than one wife. Some men had six wives; most took only two because supporting them was expensive. Interestingly, the second wife was often the younger sister of the first. In fact, upon marriage to the first wife, a man was given rights to her younger sisters. If he could not support them then but felt he might like to have them in the future, he could forbid their marriage to other men. If the younger sister had another suitor, one whom she wished to marry, she invited him to take—abduct—her from the home of her guardians. In this case, the suitor's family gave the wedding feast, inviting her guardians. If they came to the feast, it showed they favored the union.

Although not as common as polygamy, the Sioux also practiced polyandry, the taking of multiple husbands. Walker maintains, "In nearly every instance of plural husbands there was no offspring by the first husband, yet the couple were congenial and wished to live as man and wife. The second husband was taken that there might be children and such children were considered the children of the original

pair."[32] The second husband had no say in family policy and no status as a father. However, the begetting of offspring was in itself a measure of status. To the Sioux, the birth of a child was a highly important event.

Birth and Death

The life of a nomad was harsh, and many Sioux children did not live to see their first year. Because of this and because the Sioux loved their children with a fierceness akin to that manifested in battle, the birth of a child was a joyous affair. From the moment a woman announced her pregnancy to the time her offspring was born, preparations were intense. The mother or grandmother prepared a decorated bag in the shape of a lizard or tortoise to hold the child's umbilical cord, which was believed to contain the baby's entity or self. The sisters of the father were responsible for making cradles for the baby. The more elaborate the cradle and the more cradles received, the more esteemed their brother's wife.

The birth was conducted according to custom. A strong stake was pounded into the ground. The expectant mother squatted beside this, holding its top with both hands while cramps washed over her. When the child was born, it was caught on a soft piece of deerskin. The newborn was washed with damp braids of sweet grass and oiled in buffalo grease. The umbilical cord was given special attention. It was pulled through a spherical puff ball (a type of fungi), sprinkled with its spores, and

The birth of a child is considered a momentous occasion in Sioux culture.

then tucked within the puff ball and bound tightly to the baby's body. The mother's afterbirth, the placenta that nourished the baby while in the womb, was wrapped in hide and placed high in a tree.

When the baby was four days old, a naming ceremony was held. This ceremony began with a "giveaway," the typical Sioux demonstration of generosity. The parents gave away many gifts, primarily to the very poor and the very powerful. A feast was held for the mother, after which the father told the name of the child. Some were named after a grandparent, others after the father's bravest exploit or his most powerful vision. Some fathers asked a *winkte*, a Sioux man who assumed a woman's role and duties, to give the child a secret name, one that could never be spoken. Because *winktes* did not fight or hunt, they were long-lived, so this secret name ensured the child's longevity. Another method of ascertaining a long life for a girl was to set a date for the ear-piercing ritual. By setting this date for the following summer, the girl would be certain to live through the first dangerous year.

The disadvantage to being a people so full of love for one another was that the grief upon losing a friend or relative was shattering. Their burial customs enabled them to cope, though. In her book *Red Man's Religion,* author Ruth M. Underhill describes these customs:

> The Sioux, untouched by fear, maintained a kind of companionship with their dead. . . . Sioux mourners proclaimed their grief by passionate wailing, by lacerating their arms and legs, and even by cutting off a finger joint.

> The Sioux caressed the bones of their dead and kept them where they could be visited. . . . The corpses were laid on platforms under which kin might sit for days, the women wailing, the men silently brooding. Later, the relatives might remove the skulls and lay them in a circle, with a buffalo skull as guard. There women have been seen to sit by the hour, talking to their lost ones.[33]

The Sioux placed their graves high on platforms because when they prayed they raised their hands and faces to the Great Spirit, Wakan Tanka. In this manner, and in most others, the Sioux's customs were entwined, even based on, their religion.

Wakan Tanka

The Sioux religion celebrated the tribe's union with nature. Wakan Tanka, creator of the universe and all within it, was worshiped above all. In prayer, Wakan Tanka was addressed as "Father" and "Grandfa-

Half-Men or Winkte

There was one other class of Sioux individual, not wholly man nor completely female: the *winkte.* These were men who dressed like women, acted like women, and performed the duties of women. They were outcasts in Sioux society, forced to place their tepees at the outer edge of the camp and viewed with both contempt and fear. Because they did not assume the highly dangerous male role, they were called sissies and held in contempt by the average Sioux male. However, because they were called to the role of half-men by a dream, they were also feared because of their great holiness and power. For this reason, the Sioux tolerated their presence.

In addition to their sacred powers, these half-men served as healers. They were also called on to give sacred names to children, secretive names that none may speak aloud. *Winktes* were known for their sense of humor, and it showed in many of the secret names given. It would take a good sense of humor to be a half-man in the Sioux society.

ther," but he was not necessarily one god. He was one god who was four. The Sioux placed great stock in the number four. Wakan Tanka had four names: Chief God, the Great Spirit, the Creator, and the Executive. He was creator of the four directions. The buffalo came from the west, wisdom from the east, a bracing cold wind from the north, and warmth from the south.

Historian John Upton Terrell lists a number of other fours significant to the Sioux and central to their worship of Wakan Tanka and his creations:

> There were four elements above the earth: the sky, the sun, the moon, the stars. There were four parts of time: the day, the night, the month, the year. There were four phases of man's life: infancy, childhood, maturity, old age. There were four parts to all plants: roots, stem, leaves, fruit. There were four classes of animals: crawling, flying, two-legged, four-legged.
>
> And so there were four virtues which all men were expected to seek: bravery, fortitude, generosity and wisdom.[34]

After placing their dead on high platforms, family members would often visit the site and bring gifts for the deceased.

The number four was occasionally multiplied with the important number seven. For example, there are twenty-eight days in one moon, or the Sioux month. The buffalo has twenty-eight ribs. The Oglala holy man Black Elk reports that the lodge used in the sun dance ceremony was constructed of twenty-eight exterior poles. Four, seven, and twenty-eight were numbers of great significance to the Sioux.

Ceremonial Equipment

The Sioux religious ceremonies were conducted with ritualistic dignity, using drums, tobacco, sage, sweet grass, and a pipe. Black Elk explains the symbolism of the drum: "The round form of the drum represents the whole universe, and its steady strong beat is the pulse, the heart, throbbing at the center of the universe. It is as the voice of Wakan Tanka, and this

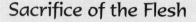

Sacrifice of the Flesh

To be given a vision was to have been singled out for favor by Wakan Tanka, so the Sioux actively sought conditions conducive to vision reception. They did not use hallucinatory drugs like some other tribes, preferring instead to reduce their physical well-being to a weakened state where hallucinations, or visions, were more likely to occur. For this reason, many of their religious ceremonies involved prolonged fasting or excessive exertion leading to exhaustion. They also courted extreme pain through the sacrifice of the flesh portion of the sun dance ritual.

There were three primary methods of sacrificing flesh. The most common was to be fastened to the sun dance lodge center pole and then dance while attempting to free oneself. Bone skewers were shoved through the flesh on the chest and tied to the top of the pole. As the warrior danced, he leaned backwards, straining against the

pole. Usually the flesh tore, and he was freed. Sometimes he passed out before he could free himself, or he did not possess the strength to free himself. When this happened, helpers gave him a good shove until he was freed.

These skewers could also be placed in the flesh on the warrior's back. They were then tied to buffalo skulls, which the dancer dragged around the sun dance lodge until they tore loose. Reports are made of warriors dragging as many as twelve buffalo skulls at one time.

Slices of flesh, generally taken from the arms, was another offering to Wakan Tanka. After a long fast and before the sun dance, helpers sliced strips of skin and flesh from the warrior's arms. Often the warrior passed out before the conclusion of the dance, and it was in this state of extreme pain and exhaustion that most visions occurred.

sound stirs us and helps us to understand the mystery and power of all things."[35] The Sioux often referred to their people as "the sacred hoop" of the universe, a circle with no beginning, no end, and Wakan Tanka at its center.

The tobacco used by the Sioux in their ceremonies was a combination of dried tree bark called kinnikinnick, regular tobacco, and herbs or roots for fragrance. The smoke it emitted helped the Sioux communicate with Wakan Tanka. Sage could be used for sitting or resting on during an especially grueling ceremony. The sweet grass was either burned or used to wipe the sacred pipe, the most important of all religious equipment.

When the Sioux prayed to the Great Spirit, they called on all of his creations. These creations, in the form of a pinch of tobacco, were placed in the sacred pipe. Mother Earth might be called on to pray with the supplicant, and a pinch of sacred tobacco representing her was placed in the pipe. Then the wingeds, the two-leggeds, and the four-leggeds might be called on, one at a time, and also placed in the pipe. When the pipe was filled with the creations of Wakan Tanka, it was lit and, after first offering the smoke to the four directions and then to the sky and the earth, smoked. In

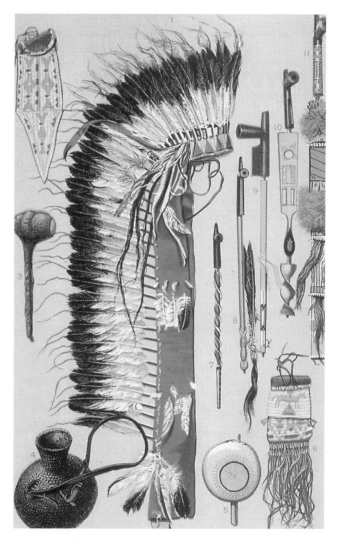

Sioux ceremonies used a variety of items, including elaborate headdresses, pipes decorated with an assortment of feathers and beads, jars, and other items of clothing.

this manner, the supplicant prayed *to* the creations and *with* the creations, worshiping them even as he or she called on their aid in worshiping Wakan Tanka. This ensured the strongest possible prayer.

The Sacred Hoop Game

The Sioux loved to play games. Many of their games had their basis in religious ceremony, as in the case of the sacred hoop game. In this game, a large wooden hoop was rolled across the ground while two men competed to knock it over with special throwing sticks. It is not enough to merely knock the hoop over, though. The hoop must land on the throwing sticks, touching only the nonwood portions, such as the thong tying them together, or the rawhide strip around their centers.

The sacred hoop game had woodland origins. According to tradition, a band of Sioux was facing starvation. They had seen no buffalo for a long time, and they were weak from hunger. One night a young man was given the sacred hoop game in a vision. The hoop and sticks were prepared in a highly sacred manner, utilizing sweet grass and sage. When this first hoop was rolled, everyone was surprised to see that it left hoofprints in the dirt. The young dreamer informed them that in four days four buffalo would walk through the camp. He warned them that the buffalo must not be harmed.

Four days later, four buffalo appeared. The starving band members had great respect for the *wakan* young man and did not bother the buffalo. Shortly after this, a massive herd of buffalo was sighted, and the people were finally able to eat.

The Sioux enjoyed the sacred hoop game and centuries later were still playing it for fun.

The sacred hoop game was a form of entertainment as well as a reminder of previous spiritual experiences.

The Seven Rites of the White Buffalo Cow Woman

Lakota tradition states that the first sacred pipe was given to the Sioux by a beautiful woman. Long ago two warriors were approached by a lovely maiden. One leered at her and had impure thoughts. The other was afraid and cautioned his friend that the woman was *wakan,* meaning "holy and powerful." His friend did not listen and was turned into a worm-riddled skeleton. The good man took the woman to his camp, where she gave the people the first sacred pipe and instructions for its use. She also promised to reveal to them seven sacred rites that they must practice. Upon leaving, she turned into a lovely white buffalo cow.

One of the seven rites revealed was ghost-keeping, a ceremony allowing grieving parents to hold on to a dead child's spirit. "The Sioux believed," states Underhill, "in four souls, three of which died with the body. The fourth could be kept for a while by a loving family in the form of a 'spirit bundle.'"[36] A lock of hair was clipped from the deceased child, wrapped in buckskin, and kept in the tepee of its parents. The environment of the tepee must be pure, so the father could not argue nor kill so much as a buffalo. After a year, the child's spirit was released.

Another ritual was the purification rite, or *inipi,* which took place in the Sioux sweat lodge, the closest thing the Sioux had to a church. Even its construction was in keeping with religious precepts. Black Elk calls this rite "very *wakan*" and says it is "used before any great undertaking for which we wish to make ourselves pure or for which we wish to gain strength. . . . From this we received much of our power."[37] In the purification rite, steam was created by pouring water on hot rocks, the sacred pipe was smoked, and prayer was offered.

There was also the vision quest rite. This ritual was held on a mountaintop, preferably in the sacred Black Hills, or Paha Sapa. There, the supplicant fasted, walked, smoked, prayed, and sang while calling on the Great Spirit for guidance. If lucky, Wakan Tanka gave him or her a vision. This vision, later interpreted by a holy man, might contain lifestyle rules, instructions for the future, or knowledge of secret powers, and it sometimes resulted in a new name. Black Elk calls the vision quest "lamenting," saying, "The most important reason for 'lamenting' is that it helps us to realize our oneness with all things, to know that all things are our relatives; and then in behalf of all things we pray to *Wakan-Tanka* that He may give us knowledge of Him who is the source of all things, yet greater than all things."[38]

The Sun Dance

The most famous of the seven rites was the sun dance. This was held each June or July "when the moon is full," according to Black Elk, "for the growing and dying of the moon reminds us of our ignorance which comes and goes; but when the moon is full it is as if the eternal light of

Chapter 5

The White Man Cometh: From Fur Traders to the Settlers

Whenever two cultures meet, neither is left unaffected. Generally the least advanced of the two cultures is affected to the largest extent. The coming of the white man forever altered the ways of the Sioux. Although the Sioux were contemptuous of the European-descended interloper, they admired his technology. His weapons were superior. His iron made excellent knives and lethal tips for their arrows. His wool blankets, as warm as a buffalo robe, were brightly colored. His paints were smooth and vivid; his beads and buttons shiny and brilliant. Once introduced to these standards of white civilization, the Sioux were consumed with desire.

As for the white man, he desired something only the Native American could give him in the quantities he required for resale: furs. The Upper Great Plains teemed with animals bearing the rich coats desired by the American and European markets. Beaver was especially prized, but there was also a big demand for thick russet buffalo robes. The demand for these was so high that it could not possibly be satisfied by the first white hunters to enter Sioux territory. It was far easier to trade for them.

The Native Americans wanted the technology of the Europeans; the Europeans wanted the furs abounding on the northern Great Plains. A mutually advantageous relationship began.

The Fur Trade

Not all of the Sioux were willing to trade, though. When Meriwether Lewis and William Rogers Clark made their famous 1804 expedition to the Upper Great Plains, they made careful notes in their journals about each tribe. Of the Seven Council Fires, Lewis reported that the four Dakota tribes were amenable toward trade, as were the northern Yankton. Once they reached the Missouri River, though, they noticed a deterioration in attitudes. Of the Yanktonai, Lewis noted that this tribe liked to trade but tended to do so forcefully, setting their own prices for their goods.

Lewis reserved his strongest language, however, for the Teton, calling them "the vilest miscreants [villains] of the savage race," and stating that "persuasion or advice, with them, is viewed as supplication, and only tends to inspire them with contempt for those who offer either."[41] The Lakota wanted the white man's goods, but they were reluctant to deal with him. They preferred to attend the annual spring fairs held by the allies. At these fairs, they traded horses and buffalo robes with the other tribes for "considerable quantities of arms, ammunition, axes, knives, kettles, cloth, and a variety of other articles,"[42] according to Lewis. Using the Dakota and Nakota as middlemen, the Teton were able to obtain the goods they desired. In time, however, they also openly engaged in trade with the whites.

At first the relationship between the traders and the Sioux was a good one. The Sioux's lifestyle, though greatly improved by the white man's goods, remained much the same. The traders made a good living selling the furs and robes, and many of them adopted Sioux ways and married Sioux women. Then both parties became

Trade between Indians and whites was initially beneficial for both groups, until both parties became greedy.

greedy. The fur traders wanted more and more furs, and the Sioux "became increasingly reliant on European trade goods,"[43] according to author David J. Wishart. The emphasis of Sioux hunting became trade, not food, shelter, and clothing.

The Domino Effect

This change in emphasis marked the beginning of what would become an overall subversion of Sioux customs. It had what is called a domino effect. Stack dominoes on their ends in a long row and knock the first one over. All of the following dominoes will fall in rapid succession. So it was when the Sioux began killing for trade, with the row of dominoes representing various aspects of their culture.

The men began to spend more time hunting and the women more time preparing hides, which meant both had less time for traditional activities. The men took more wives to keep up with the workload. Worse, the Sioux became major players in the decimation of the buffalo. George E. Hyde contends that the Indians of the Great Plains were responsible for 105,000 buffalo cow deaths in 1847 alone. Sioux hunters also learned to kill wantonly. Reports were made of over 1,500 buffalo slain by Sioux who took only the tongues for trade and of Oglala hunters taking only their favorite sections of meat and leaving the rest of the buffalo carcasses for predators.

Perhaps the heftiest dominoes, falling with resounding thuds, came with the introduction of alcohol and disease. The Sioux were unaccustomed to alcohol, and once introduced to liquor, many craved it. This addiction spawned ugly changes. Murder became common. Some men became beggars at the trading posts. The Sioux realized alcohol was harmful but lacked the strength to resist it. Nor could they resist the diseases carried unwittingly by the fur traders. Cholera, smallpox, and measles epidemics swept through their bands, killing indiscriminately. The survivors of these epidemics would pass on to their children their resistance, but the first generation paid with thousands of lives.

The dominoes were falling, one after another, toppling the Sioux culture. Still the Sioux's thirst for the white man's trade goods was strong. Because of this, the final domino, the lease or outright sale of Mother Earth, would be set in motion.

Treaties

By the mid-1800s the fur trade had begun to wane. Many of the animals had been overhunted, and some types of furs were no longer in demand. The fur traders moved on, telling mouth-watering stories of the wealth in land, timber, and minerals in Sioux territory. When U.S. citizens became anxious to have this land, the United States tried to buy or lease it. It offered money, set-aside lands known as reservations for the displaced Sioux, and yearly "annuities," which consisted of cash and food, placing these conditions of purchase into written agreements known as treaties. It could not see how the Sioux could refuse, which is a good example of the chasm existing between the two cultures.

The introduction of alcohol proved to be the downfall of many Sioux men who could not resist its addiction.

The Sioux believed that the land, like themselves, was one of Wakan Tanka's creations, not a possession to be bought or sold. The white men, on the other hand, believed land was the foremost of all possessions.

Despite this, the U.S. government sent representatives to make treaties with the Sioux. Because the Sioux could not read, treaties were read to them. Because they could not write, they "touched the pen" to agree, and their name was signed for them. The Lakota signed one of these agreements in 1851. The Oregon Trail, an overland route leading to the West Coast, had been blazed by then. The immigrants be-

gan steering their wagons along its northern leg, through Lakota territory. When the Teton raided these wagon trains, either robbing the immigrants or making them pay a fee for crossing their land, the immigrants complained loudly to their government. It responded with a treaty promising the Lakota annuities. In return it asked them not to attack the immigrants and to give the U.S. military the right to construct forts in Lakota territory.

Although this was not the first peace agreement signed by the Sioux, it was the first important treaty signed by the Lakota. By allowing the military to move into their territory and by accepting annuities, the

Lakota took the first step in initiating close, often daily contact with the white invaders. Agencies under the protection of the U.S. military were established for the distribution of annuity goods, and camp selection was often based on the proximity of the nearest agency. Annuity goods were more predictable and easier to procure than buffalo, and some Sioux became wholly dependent on the white man, hunting only rarely. These Sioux lost much of the old ways and were called "agency Indians" or "tame Indians."

The presence of the military also posed a problem. The U.S. soldiers stationed at the agencies based their opinion of the Sioux on the agency Indians. Unaware that the majority of the Lakota either refused annuities or came in only once a year to collect them, the soldiers judged all Sioux by the actions of the tame Sioux and became contemptuous of the entire nation. In 1854 this attitude led to the first skirmish in what would prove to be two decades of sporadic on-again, off-again Sioux wars. Lieutenant Grattan, stationed at Fort

General William T. Sherman at the signing of a treaty that ended Red Cloud's War at Fort Laramie, Wyoming, in 1868.

U.S. Soldiers

Some of the Sioux's difficulties with the U.S. government stemmed from the type of men who chose a soldier's life. After the Civil War, most men had had their fill of war. Those who volunteered to continue serving their country were, therefore, a special type. Some were racists. A few liked killing. Most enjoyed war as much as or more than the Sioux. In his book *Red Cloud's Folks,* author George E. Hyde describes the typical Indian fighter.

"The Colorado cavalry and other troops recruited on the frontier regarded the Indians as wild animals and thought nothing of killing them, and many of the soldiers from the East soon developed this attitude. Lieutenant Eugene F. Ware tells us that the Kansas troops at Camp Cottonwood on the lower Platte [River], wishing to have a bit of practice with their artillery, dropped a number of shells on a party of Sioux Indians who were seen on an island in the river. This happened before there was any trouble, the Indians being perfectly friendly. In the *Life of Caspar Collins,* by A. W. Spring, we find this youthful officer dwelling on the eagerness with which the men and officers of his regiment, the Eleventh Ohio Cavalry, looked forward to an opportunity to show what they could do in an Indian fight. These Ohio men, stationed along the North Platte with headquarters at Fort Laramie, were listening enviously to the tales of the frontiersmen. Most of the soldiers soon discarded their uniforms, decking themselves out in buckskins, moccasins, and Spanish spurs, and having provided themselves with hardy Indian ponies out of their own pay they awaited eagerly a chance to exhibit their prowess as Indian fighters."

Laramie in what is now the state of Wyoming, tried to enforce the white man's law in a large encampment of Lakota. Although he had with him only thirty men, he fired on the Lakota, and he and his men were killed. Grattan was the first to mistake all Sioux for tame Indians, but he would not be the last.

The Minnesota Uprising

While the Lakota were signing this first important treaty, their eastern allies, the Dakota, were signing a treaty of their own. By the mid-1800s, Minnesota was thick with settlers who had for decades been bullying the Santee. In 1851 the desperate Dakota tribes signed away 24 million acres of prime Minnesota land, moving to two tiny reservations. For their land they were promised less than seven cents an acre and annuities for fifty years. When they did not receive their money, the Dakota were angry, claiming that the 1851 treaty had not been read to them correctly. They were somewhat appeased at the thought of the upcoming annuities, but the men in charge of the Santee agencies, the Indian agents, kept those for themselves. Unable to hunt or fish their old land and cheated

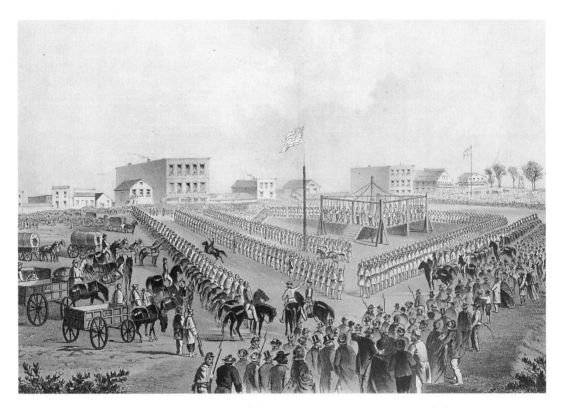

Spectators gather for the hanging of thirty-nine Santee warriors who led an uprising that resulted in at least eight hundred dead settlers in Minnesota in 1862.

out of their annuities by dishonest agents, it was not long before the Santee began to simmer with resentment.

In 1862 things came to a boil. "The winter of 1861–62 was one of near starvation for the Santee," writes historian John Upton Terrell. "In desperate condition, they looked forward to June, when goods and cash annuities were due to be given them. Nothing came in June. Nothing came in July. Nothing came in August."[44] The starving Dakota could take no more. The Mdewakanton leader Little Crow is credited with leading what was the bloodiest en-

gagement in the Sioux wars. In August the Santee began sacking the Minnesota countryside. Minnesota's Sixth Regiment took a week to arrive to the aid of the southern settlers. By that time at least eight hundred whites were dead. The Dakota uprising did not last long after the arrival of the Sixth Regiment, though. Faced with superior numbers and superior weapons, the Dakota surrendered by the end of September. Thirty-nine Santee were hanged and another three hundred were imprisoned.

Not all of the Dakota surrendered, however. Some, including Little Crow, fled to

Canada. Other Santee warriors fled to their allies on the prairies. The Lakota listened to the tale they told and became determined to avoid their fate.

Red Cloud's War

One who may have listened was the Oglala headman Red Cloud. As a young boy Red Cloud had seen his father die after drinking cheap alcohol, so he had no love for the white man. When new gold fields were discovered in the state of Montana and the Lakota were asked to sign a treaty ensuring safe passage for the miners, Red Cloud refused. This made him popular with his people, and he became leader of the Oglala Sioux. As a result, the

Little Crow's Final Defeat

In June 1863 Little Crow made the mistake of returning to Minnesota to steal some horses. He may have been unaware that, in the aftermath of the Dakota uprising, the state of Minnesota had begun offering a twenty-five-dollar bounty for Santee scalps. While picking raspberries, Little Crow was shot and killed by settlers hunting deer. When the hunters realized they had shot the leader of the rebellion, they exacted revenge on Little Crow's corpse, scalping it, mutilating it, and burying it in a pile of cow dung.

Sioux achieved one of the few Native American victories over the United States.

The success of Red Cloud's warriors lay in their tactics. Red Cloud knew they could not mount a full-scale offensive against the superior might of the U.S. military. He chose instead to fight them as Sioux. Using small raiding parties, Red Cloud's men were like a bee stinging the great exposed flesh of the whites. They dove in to attack wagon trains and were quickly away before troops could come to the rescue. They harassed the road-building crews. The military constructed three forts along the trail, but the forts became prisons for the troops within. One soldier, Lieutenant William Fetterman, boasted that with eighty men he could ride unmolested through Sioux territory. In December 1866 he was given his wish and immediately fell prey to the Sioux decoy trick. Hastily pursuing a few Oglala warriors, one of whom went by the name of Crazy Horse, Fetterman rounded a corner to face a massive war party. He and his eighty men died.

For the first time, the U.S. government realized what the Sioux could do when organized into one people with one voice. That voice told the U.S. government to remove its troops from Lakota territory, and in 1868 the United States did just that. In November Red Cloud finally signed a treaty with the whites. This treaty gave the Sioux all of the South Dakota land west of the Missouri River, a territory including the Black Hills. However, the United States did not know then that Paha Sapa was rich in gold.

Under Red Cloud's leadership, the Sioux were successful in obtaining concessions from the U.S. government.

Black Hills Gold

In 1874 the United States heard that there was gold in the Black Hills and sent an expedition to look into the matter. The Sioux were uneasy when they learned who was leading the expedition: Lieutenant Colonel George Armstrong Custer, long a thorn in the Indian's side. When Custer's expedition reported unimaginable wealth, gold-hungry whites converged on the Black Hills. The United States ordered its military to evict the miners, but the military could not control these citizens. By 1875 it quit trying. The United States decided it would be easier to purchase Paha Sapa.

Red Cloud was by this time an agency Indian and was more concerned with personal grievances than with the Black Hills. Therefore, many of the Sioux chose to ally themselves with a group known as the Powder River Hostiles. According to George E. Hyde, "The northern group of Tetons, led by the fierce Hunkpapas, had been unfriendly as far back as 1856, and when the Minnesota Sioux came into their country in 1862 they allied themselves with them and became bitterly hostile."[45] When U.S. delegates arrived to negotiate the purchase of the Black Hills, members of these hostile factions made their job a risky affair.

Ultimately, the Sioux refused to sell, and by the time this council concluded, the U.S. delegates were unhappy with the way they had been treated. They reported that no agreement could be reached with the Sioux. The United States was displeased. In its opinion, it had tried peace. Now it was time for war. That winter the United States ordered all of the Sioux to the reservations, giving them until January 31, 1876, to comply. This was not much time, but that did not matter. Both parties were ready for war.

The Hunkpapa holy man Sitting Bull called a great council in April, asking Sioux, Cheyenne, and Arapaho warriors to join his tribe's fight against the whites. Thousands responded. On June 14, 1876, a sun dance was held, and during the ritual Sitting Bull had fifty pieces of flesh cut from his arms. He then danced until he collapsed from exhaustion. In his reduced physical state, he had a great vision. Hundreds of white soldiers fell from the sky.

These soldiers fell headfirst, a very promising sign. When the Lakota next fought, they did so with absolute confidence in Wakan Tanka's blessing.

The first fight occurred three days later. The United States had sent three columns of troops into Lakota territory hoping to attack the Sioux simultaneously from the east, west, and south. On June 17 General George Crook's northbound column encountered Sioux and Cheyenne forces led by the Oglala leader Crazy Horse, who yelled, "Come on, Lakotas, it's a good day to die!" The Indians were in a strong position and could have won. "But eventually the individualistic nature of the Sioux and Cheyenne warriors began to assert itself,"

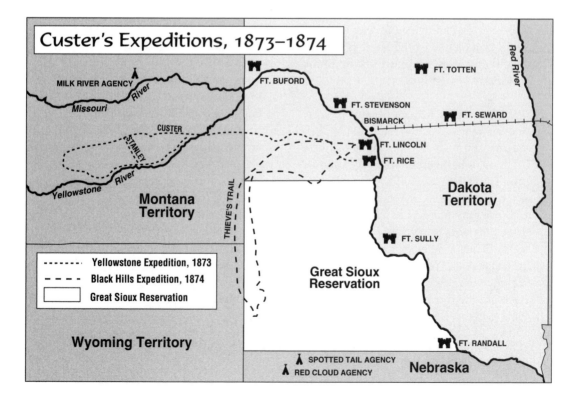

Custer's Expeditions, 1873–1874

MILK RIVER AGENCY
Missouri River
FT. BUFORD
FT. TOTTEN
Red River
FT. STEVENSON
BISMARCK
FT. SEWARD
CUSTER
STANLEY River
FT. LINCOLN
FT. RICE
Yellowstone River
Montana Territory
THIEVE'S TRAIL
Dakota Territory
FT. SULLY
- - - - - - - Yellowstone Expedition, 1873
- - - - Black Hills Expedition, 1874
☐ Great Sioux Reservation
Great Sioux Reservation
Wyoming Territory
FT. RANDALL
SPOTTED TAIL AGENCY
RED CLOUD AGENCY
Nebraska

explains historian Ralph K. Andrist. "Early in the afternoon they started to break off fighting and to drift away. . . . One of the warriors explained it later, 'They were tired and hungry, so they went home.'"[46] Crook's troops suffered severe losses and sat out the Sioux wars for the rest of that summer.

The Battle of the Little Bighorn

The leaders of the other two columns, Colonel John Gibbon and Major General Alfred H. Terry, pushed onward. Among the divisions commanded by Terry was the

Little Big Man

Emotions ran high at the Black Hills Council. The Sioux were divided into two factions, those who were considering the U.S. government's wishes and those who were not. The government's representatives, guarded only by a small contingent of troopers, were uneasy and on more than one occasion had reason to fear for their lives. An example of the latter is beautifully depicted by George E. Hyde in his book *Red Cloud's Folks*.

"Presently the excitement became greater; an opening was made in the circle of warriors and through the opening shot Little Big Man, a belligerent young gentleman from Crazy Horse's wild camp. He was naked and mounted on the bare back of a fine iron gray pony, with a lariat knotted around the pony's lower jaw in place of a bridle. In one hand he clutched a Winchester, and his other fist was full of cartridges. Riding toward the tent, he announced in a voice like the roar of a cannon that he had come to kill the white men who were trying to take his land. A number of Oglala soldiers surrounded him, snatched his gun,

and amid immense confusion and excitement removed him from the circle. The warriors were riding up and down making little dashes (they always did before a fight), and some of the leaders were yelling *Hoka hey!* (the call for a charge). . . .

Suddenly there was a wild rush of mounted Sioux toward the commission; but the warriors charged past the tent and up to Egan's troop, who were sitting on their horses with their carbines gripped in their hands. It was now seen that this was no hostile movement; it was Young-Man-Afraid-of-His-Horse and his Oglala soldiers. Hearing the Indians yelling for a charge, he had rushed his men in and formed a screen between Egan's troopers and the mass of infuriated Sioux. Leaving his men, he now rode into the center of the circle and shouted to the Indians to go to their lodges and not to come to council again until their heads had cooled. The Sioux knew that this man was not to be trifled with; he would kill the first man who opposed him. Band by band the warriors left the circle and rode over the hills toward their camps."

Seventh Cavalry, led by none other than Custer. Like others before him, Custer underestimated the Sioux. Terry warned him to be cautious. Likewise, his Indian scouts had warned him that a huge force of Sioux were reported to have gathered along the banks of the Little Bighorn River.

Custer listened to neither. Splitting his own regiment into four small divisions, taking with him only 225 men, he rapidly advanced on what was "the largest concentration of Indians ever assembled at one place within the area of the United States,"[47] according to author Angie Debo. As Custer raced up the ridge overlooking the Indian encampment, his thoughts were probably on the glory that would be his. Once he reached the summit and saw the thousands of lodges below, it can be assumed that he immediately recognized his error.

This camp was led by the cream of the Lakota warriors: Sitting Bull, Crazy Horse, Gall, and many more of like valor. Although they were surprised by the attack, it did not take these great leaders long to spring into action. As Custer and the 225 members of his Seventh Cavalry raced toward the camp, they were engulfed by a swarm of Sioux and Cheyenne warriors. The battle did not last long. Sitting

Crazy Horse was one of the warriors who led the Sioux to victory at the Battle of the Little Bighorn.

Bull is reported to have said that it lasted only as long as it takes a white man to eat his breakfast. Custer and his men dismounted and fought standing. They attempted to shield themselves with their horses, but it is difficult to hold a fright-

Crazy Horse Monument

Mount Rushmore, a monument to four of the greatest U.S. presidents, erupts in the heart of the Black Hills. The Sioux consider these busts a blasphemous stain on their sacred Paha Sapa. In 1947, in response to this national landmark, Lakota chief Standing Bear asked sculptor Korczak Ziolkowski to create another sculpture, this one honoring the greatest of all Lakota warriors, Crazy Horse. Ziolkowski had worked on the Mount Rushmore sculpture, so he knew what he was tackling when he agreed to do the job. He traveled through the Black Hills, seeking the right spot for the sculpture and settling on an enormous granite cliff on Thunderhead Mountain. Ziolkowski dreamed big. This sculpture would not be a bust—the Crazy Horse Monument would be a full figure of the man and his horse. When finished, it would be ten times the size of Mount Rushmore.

Ziolkowski devoted his life to the work. He told his wife and children that the sculpture came first, and they worked beside him, blasting and carving a mountain into a man. When he died in 1982, Ziolkowski's children took over, carrying on their father's dream, which is still in progress. In 1997, fifty years after work had begun, the face of Crazy Horse was revealed to an awe-struck audience, and a ceremonial first dynamite blast was made on the horse the Sioux leader rides. It is uncertain when the monument will be completed. Perhaps a third generation of Ziolkowskis will be needed to see the work to completion. However, once finished, the statue of Crazy Horse will be the only monument of its dimensions in the world.

ened horse while firing a weapon, so most fought exposed. When the dust cleared, Custer and all of his men were dead.

The Cessation of Hostilities

The Battle of the Little Bighorn occurred on June 25, 1876. By the time the rest of the Seventh Cavalry made it to the nearest communications center, it was July 5. The news of the battle, therefore, was reported to the United States on the day after its great centennial celebration. One hundred years before, the nation's founding fathers had declared independence from British rule. Now their descendants were dying at the hands of "savages." In the history of the Indian wars, only one tribe had managed to annihilate U.S. forces three times. There was Grattan, then Fetterman, and now Custer. Always it was the Sioux. The public outcry was fierce: Something must be done about the Sioux.

The United States retaliated quickly and thoroughly. Throughout the rest of 1876 and most of 1877, the U.S. military was unceasing in its efforts to punish the Powder River Hostiles. Crazy Horse and his band were

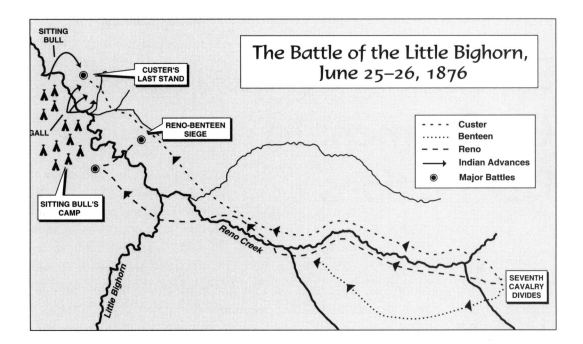

The Battle of the Little Bighorn, June 25–26, 1876

barely able to set up camp before the military found them once again, and in 1877 Crazy Horse surrendered. When he rebelled at confinement to a jail cell, he was bayoneted by a tribal policeman. Sitting Bull fled to Canada, where he remained with his Hunkpapa Sioux until 1881. He toured with Buffalo Bill's Wild West Show from 1885 to 1889 before settling down to reservation life with the rest of the once great Sioux Nation.

The citizens of the United States were pleased. Something had finally been done about the Sioux.

Chapter 6

Elimination of "Siouxness": Confinement to Reservations

It is a common practice for conquering nations to strip those that they have conquered of their cultural identity. This dissolves the glue that binds a people together, forcing them to accept and assume the cultural heritage of the victors. In theory, this practice, called forced assimilation, eases the transition for the conquered people. It also forestalls the possibility of future rebellion. By denying the Sioux all that made them Sioux, the United States could be certain they would never again rise to power.

In first forcing assimilation on the Sioux, the United States was aided by "sportsmen" and hunters. By 1883 the basis of the Sioux economy—the buffalo— had been all but destroyed. Parties of sportsmen had ridden the new railroads through buffalo country, wantonly shooting the massive beasts from the comfort of their Pullman cars and leaving a trail of carcasses in their wake. The buffalo hunters had killed the rest. According to

author Robert M. Utley, "In 1871 an eastern tannery hit upon buffalo hides as a source of commercial leather. By the hundreds 'hide hunters' spread over the Plains, slaughtering the buffalo at the rate of three million a year. . . . By 1883 a scientific expedition could find only two hundred buffalo in all the west."[48]

Gone was the hunt, with its ceremony and opportunities for status. Gone was the means to trade or to keep their families fed and clothed. The Sioux became wholly dependent on the white man, spending his money, eating his food, and wearing his clothing. Gone were the tepee and the camp circle. The Sioux were issued cheap government housing, and their family structure became nuclear, not extended. Ultimately, gone was the purpose for a nomadic life. The Sioux were confined to reservations and had to learn to live in one location. The destruction of the buffalo shattered the Sioux culture, but it proved only the beginning.

Forced Assimilation

Assimilation could not be accomplished merely by taking away the Sioux lifestyle and livelihood. Now that the Sioux were living like whites, they needed to be taught to think like whites. This meant they needed to be stripped of their "Siouxness," of the customs that made them think like Sioux. This job was undertaken by the Bureau of Indian Affairs (BIA). When the Sioux submitted to reservation confinement, they were placed under control of the federal government. The BIA is the government branch concerned with regulating reservation societies, and it worked ceaselessly to encourage a rapid assimilation of the Sioux.

The giveaway, that Sioux demonstration of generosity, was banned. Polygamy was outlawed, as was polyandry. The men were forced to give up all wives but one, a hardship both for the man who had to choose and for the wife (or wives) not chosen. They were strongly encouraged to cut their hair and to dress in the fashion of their conquerors. They were taught to farm and ranch. Their religion was taken from them. As historian David Hurst Thomas writes, "In 1883, the Bureau of Indian Affairs further insinuated itself into the Indian heart and home by issuing throughout its growing reservation network a circular entitled *The Code of Religious Offenses.*"[49] All religious ceremonies were declared taboo, including the seven rites given by the White Buffalo Cow Woman. Any Sioux caught practicing the old religion was punished, either by a withholding of rations or by imprisonment.

Assimilation is a lengthy process. The Sioux culture had been centuries in the making, and the United States could see that it would take

Forced to wear white man's clothing was one way that the Sioux were assimilated into white society.

a very long time to eliminate Siouxness in the adults. However, if it could prevent the children from ever learning their heritage, it could assimilate the Sioux in one generation. The government began taking the children from their homes at a young age, sending them to boarding schools hundreds, even thousands, of miles away.

There, the children's hair was cut, and they were dressed as whites. They were taught the white man's ways and the white man's history. They were forbidden to speak their native language. They were beaten for behaving as Sioux. They were denied visits home. Some children did not see their parents for over a decade. The BIA enjoyed great success with the boarding school program. When the Sioux children finally did return home, many had forgotten what it meant to be Sioux.

The Allotment Act

Another step taken by the government was the Dawes General Allotment Act. The U.S. government believed that the communal life on a reservation was too similar to

The Carlisle Indian School in Pennsylvania was one of the many boarding schools established to assimilate Sioux youth into white society.

Indian Boarding Schools

Most Native American parents were reluctant to send their children to the government boarding schools. Many hid their children when the BIA officials came to collect them. The following excerpt from Joan Smith's article "Young Once, Indian Forever," as it appears in *Native American Voices: A Reader,* depicts a Native American family surprised by unexpected visitors.

"The truck came early one August morning the summer Stella Runnels was 10. There was nothing remarkable about it. . . . But visitors were rare at the Runnels ranch, and the dozen children playing around the house ran up the dusty road to meet it.

It was only when the men with guns got out that Stella understood, in a horrified instant, what was about to happen.

'Everybody knew about the Indian boarding schools,' she says, now 70 and living with her husband on a chicken ranch in Sonoma, incredulous now as then that her family could be destroyed in a day.

'Everybody had aunties and uncles and older brothers and sisters who had been taken. I just always thought because my father was a chief in every sense of the word—he was the only person on the reservation to have 5,000 people at his funeral—I always thought because of who he was he'd be able to keep them from taking me.'

But Stella's father could not protect her from the Bureau of Indian Affairs. "The men just pointed and said, 'You, you, you, you and you,' she says. 'They picked the five of us with the best report cards. And our parents couldn't stop them because they had guns.'"

the communal life lived in Indian villages and camps. It decided that each Indian head of household should be given, allotted, 160 acres of reservation land. This would ensure that each family lived a distance from other families. This distance would destroy tribal unity, the government argued. Additionally, once the Indians learned what it was like to possess land, they would truly become white at heart.

This was what advocates of the Dawes act said. However, they had an underlying intent that was not concerned with assimilation. Many of the Sioux reservations were

so large that once each head of household was given 160 acres, there would be a great deal of leftover land. The United States planned to sell this surplus reservation land to its citizens, who were anxious to have it. Disguising its purpose as another means of helping the Sioux to adapt to their new environment, the United States set out to obtain reservation land for its citizens.

In 1887 the Dawes act was implemented. The first tribe selected to undergo the allotment process was the Dakota. According to Angie Debo, Crowded from Minnesota, they still owned about one million acres in the rich valley of the Red River of the North, in the northeastern corner of what would soon become the state of South Dakota. When allotments were completed to the two thousand Indians, the 660,000-acre "surplus" was opened to white settlement in April, 1892. [50]

As a result, the Dakota reservations are some of the smallest in the nation today.

Many of the Teton Sioux resisted allotment. Again, they saw what was happening to the Santee, and they vowed it would not be repeated with them. Besides, they had already lost most of the land promised to them in the 1868 treaty. They had submitted to reservation confinement. They had accepted the destruction of the buffalo and their total dependence on annuities. They had foregone the old political and social organization. They had foregone the old generosity expressed by the giveaways. They had given up their wives and had tried farming and ranching. They had forsaken Wakan Tanka. They had stoically watched their children leave and come back, years later, thoroughly anglicized. But the United States asked too much this time. The Lakota refused to give up one more inch of their land.

The Ghost Dance

Their struggle to hold onto this land was not without cost. Had they accepted allotments, they could have leased the land and used the money to feed their children. The latter part of the nineteenth century was one of starvation for all of the Sioux, but none suffered more than the Teton. The

years 1889 and 1890 were especially bad. A drought in 1889 destroyed the Lakota's crops. "And at that very time," writes Debo, "Congress and the Indian administration cut the beef ration. The Sioux suffered from actual hunger, and when a measles epidemic struck them the following winter, their weakened children died by the hundreds."[51] The Lakota became desperate. When word came of an Indian savior in Nevada, their hunger-dulled eyes brightened with hope.

In 1889 Wovoka, a Paiute mystic, had a great vision. The time of the whites was coming to an end. In the spring of 1891, when the grass began to cover the land, all Indians would be raised up above the earth and a new layer of soil laid down, covering the whites for eternity. The buffalo and other game would return, as would all of those who had died in the struggle to hold onto their lands. The Lakota sent emissaries to learn more, and Wovoka told them what they must do to bring about this new world. Ralph K. Andrist states, "The Indians were given a special ceremonial dance, which required five successive nights to complete; the oftener they performed the dance, the more they would hasten the coming of the millennial future."[52] This dance was called the Ghost Dance. The Lakota were afraid of government reprisals if they practiced this religion, but Wovoka told them not to worry. If they wore special "ghost shirts," bullets could not harm them.

Although many Native American tribes adopted the Ghost Dance religion, none

After watching the Ghost Dance, U.S. government agents feared that the dance was a prelude to a new Sioux uprising.

tackled it with the ferocity of the Lakota. Even Red Cloud and Sitting Bull accepted the new religion. Soon the women were making ghost shirts for themselves and their families. Soon the Lakota were chanting and dancing until they dropped from exhaustion, at which time many of them had visions supportive of Wovoka's claims. And soon the U.S. government became concerned that all of this dancing was a prelude to war.

The Last Lakota "Uprising"

Its concern, however, did not extend to improving reservation conditions. The Indian agent at the Oglala Pine Ridge Reservation was angry when the U.S. government continued to send only half-rations throughout the summer of 1890. The Pine Ridge Oglala were literally starving. By the autumn of 1890, this agent could take no more, and he resigned. His replacement was a timid man who feared the Sioux. Thus began a chain of events that would culminate in one of the most shameful incidents in the history of Native American–United States relations.

The hungrier the Lakota became, the harder they danced. The harder the Lakota danced, the more they frightened their new agent. He finally begged the U.S. government to send troops to quell what he feared was a Lakota uprising, and the government responded with its best Indian fighters. Among these were the Seventh Cavalry, the same regiment that had seen 226 of its members killed in the Battle of the Little Bighorn.

It was decided that if the leaders were first dealt with, perhaps an uprising could be avoided. With this in mind, on December 15, 1890, forty-three Indian police officers were sent to arrest Sitting Bull. Tempers flared, and Sitting Bull was killed by one of the policemen. Other Lakota leaders were handled in a less inflammatory fashion until the Seventh Cavalry happened upon the band of Big Foot.

Big Foot was leading his band to the agency to collect their annuities when he was halted by two hundred members of the Seventh Cavalry. They demanded that Big Foot and his band follow them to a site on the Pine Ridge Reservation, along a creek named Wounded Knee. Once there, the soldiers sent for reinforcements, and more troops arrived. That night four hundred members of Custer's old regiment guarded

Sitting Bull's Grave

On December 17, 1890, Sitting Bull was buried in the military cemetery at Fort Yates in North Dakota, surrounded by the graves of white soldiers. He was not destined to rest there forever, however. When the military cemetery was moved in 1908, North Dakota and South Dakota began what would be a half-century tug-of-war for Sitting Bull's bones. Both states rely heavily on the money brought in by tourism, and tourists were flocking to see Sitting Bull's grave. North Dakota wanted to move Sitting Bull's grave to Bismarck. South Dakota wanted him buried on Grand River, where he had died. The War Department stepped in, telling both states to leave Sitting Bull alone. North Dakota put a concrete cover on the grave to deter grave robbers, and the matter seemed to be closed.

In 1953 Clarence Gray Eagle, Sitting Bull's nephew by marriage, led a force of Hunkpapa warriors on a daring night raid. These warriors exhumed Sitting Bull's body and removed it under the cover of darkness to a spot thirty miles south, in Mobridge, South Dakota. Burying it deep within the earth, they poured vast quantities of concrete on top, reinforcing this concrete with heavy steel rods. The governor of North Dakota was outraged but could do nothing. For the last half century, Sitting Bull's remains have finally known peace.

Big Foot's band, which consisted of over three hundred cold and hungry Lakota.

Wounded Knee

The next morning, December 29, 1890, the soldiers separated the men and older boys from the women and children and de-

The massacre of Big Foot and his band of Sioux at Wounded Knee crushed the Sioux spirit of resistance.

manded they relinquish any weapons. When only a few rifles were handed over, the Seventh Cavalry suspected deception and began searching the lodges for concealed arms. "The soldiers acted like bully-boys, overturning beds and other lodge furnishings, shoving aside the women who protested loudly and tried to bar their way,"[53] writes Andrist. Tension mounted as the men watched their women and possessions abused. Then a Lakota holy man rose and called on all to fight, reminding them of the ghost shirts many wore, shirts designed to resist bullets. It was at this point that a young Lakota man decided to use the gun he had concealed beneath his robe. Whipping out his rifle, he began firing on the U.S. soldiers.

What happened next cannot properly be called a battle. Historians—white and Indian alike—agree it was a massacre. Using only war clubs and knives, the Lakota tried to protect themselves against the Hotchkiss guns and repeating rifles of the Seventh Cavalry. This defense enraged the soldiers. Cannons boomed to the accompaniment of the staccato rhythm of repeating rifles until most of the men and older boys were dead. But the Seventh Cavalry was not satisfied. They had tasted blood, and although they had exacted some revenge for the death of Custer and his men, it was not enough. The soldiers turned on the women and children fleeing through the snow, gunning them down as they ran. Andrist aptly sums up the scene when he writes that "from the moment it opened fire, it ceased to be a military unit and became a mass of infuriated men intent only on butchery."[54]

When the smoke from the guns had cleared, a trail of corpses, mostly those of women and children, extended for two miles beyond the camp. Survivors, many of them children, were lured from their places of concealment and shot as they emerged. Debo writes that "the most careful count showed 146 dead, of whom 84 (including Big Foot) were men and boys of fighting age, 44 women, and 18 children. At least 33 were wounded, many of them mortally."[55] Other experts estimate as many as 300 Lakota killed or mortally wounded. The Seventh Cavalry claimed five dozen casualties, many of them killed by fellow soldiers in the excitement of battle.

Resolution of the "Indian Problem"

The massacre at Wounded Knee appeared to have broken the spirit of the Lakota Sioux. The mighty Teton warriors no longer existed except in legend. Conditions on the reservations continued to worsen, and all of

Mass Burial at Wounded Knee

In the aftermath of the Wounded Knee massacre, the U.S. military was faced with an unpleasant dilemma. A Great Plains blizzard had buffeted the area, driving temperatures below zero and blanketing the scene in snow. Some 150 Lakota men, women, and children lay frozen where they had fallen, many of them covered with snow. These corpses needed to be disposed of, and quickly.

The United States solved this problem by hiring civilians to dig an enormous hole in the hard winter soil. Once this cavernous pit was completed, civilians and soldiers drove through the surrounding countryside, picking up the frozen bodies and stacking them like a cord of firewood on their buck-boards. Some of the grave-digging crew plucked "souvenirs" from the corpses. Ghost shirts were especially valued. After stripping off the heavy coat the dead Lakota wore, the ghost shirt was removed and the coat replaced over the naked torso. The corpse was then tossed into the back of the wagon. Once the wagon was full, it was driven to the pit and its grisly load dumped unceremoniously within its depths.

Today that mass grave, located on the Pine Ridge Reservation, is marked by a simple white obelisk. Jutting starkly to the sky, the names of the known victims etched deeply in its side, this obelisk serves as a single headstone for the hundred-plus victims resting below.

the allies—Dakota, Nakota, and Lakota—lived in great poverty. Their children were still taken from them and reshaped through beatings. The elders continued to practice their customs, language, and religion in secrecy, but the generations to come turned more and more away from the old ways and toward alcohol as a means of shutting their hearts and souls to the hopelessness of their existence. The extended family, once the basis of the Sioux society, had become nuclear, and incidents of domestic abuse became common. On the surface, members of the Seven Council Fires were only shadows of their former selves.

Despite this bleak appearance, the United States had not finished formulating policy designed to assimilate the Native Americans. The phrase *Indian problem* had become fashionable in the nineteenth century, as in "something must be done about the Indian problem." Then it meant that the tribes must be defeated and confined to reservations or, failing that, exterminated. In the twentieth century, this phrase assumed a new, equally ominous,

meaning: The government must quit paying for the health care, feeding, and clothing of the Indians. It tried relocating young Sioux adults, offering them, in the words of David Hurst Thomas, a "bus ticket, an apartment, and an alarm clock"[56] if they were willing to leave the reservation. However, many were disillusioned by city life and returned to the reservation.

Economists then pointed to the savings that could be derived by the discontinuation of the reservation system, and a new policy was enacted, that of termination. In 1953 Congress passed a resolution addressing this new policy. According to historian Alvin M. Josephy Jr., the purpose of this resolution was in "declaring [its] intent to terminate Federal relations with the tribes."[57] Tired of meeting the financial responsibilities guaranteed by old treaties and determined to finally force assimilation on the Indians, Congress believed that termination was the answer to the Indian problem. It was unprepared, however, for the resistance it met upon implementation of this program.

Chapter 7

A New Evolution: Adaptation to Their New Environment

The massacre at Wounded Knee and all of the events preceding it dimmed the Sioux spirit but did not quench it. Beneath the appearance of dejection still coursed a genetic inheritance of extraordinary native adaptability. This genetic inheritance had enabled their nomadic ancestors to evolve from woodland Indians to Plains warriors. The eighteenth-century Sioux had not been assimilated into other Great Plains tribes. They had watched the resident tribes, adopting some of their customs, such as the use of the horse and the gun, while retaining the culture that made them Sioux. In time, they used the adopted customs to fight and overcome these resident tribes. This allowed them to adapt to their new surroundings without suffering a loss of the traditional ways, of their Siouxness. In the twentieth century, the descendants of these early warriors began striving to duplicate that feat.

Three decades after Wounded Knee, the Sioux took the first step in this direction when, in the 1920s, the Lakota sued the United States for the return of the Black Hills. It would be fifty years before the United States responded, offering the Sioux $17.5 million for the land, which they refused. The significance of this lawsuit does not lie in its unsatisfactory results or in its evidence of a movement to regain their heritage. More importantly, it demonstrated that their native adaptability was still alive. By using the legal system to fight this battle, the Sioux showed that they could learn to fight the white man using the white man's customs. It had taken them two centuries to evolve the first time. This lawsuit marked the beginning of an evolution still in progress.

Changing Attitudes

The Sioux next, perhaps unwittingly, changed the preconceived notions held by a nation. When citizens of the United States enlisted in the military to fight in World War I, Native Americans also answered the call, many of them Sioux. When these Native Americans returned home, the United States could not ignore the valor they had demonstrated in the heat of battle. According to Alvin M. Josephy Jr., "In 1924, as an acknowledgment of the country's gratitude to Indians who had volunteered for service in the armed forces during World War I, the Snyder Act conferred citizenship on all Indians."[58]

As noncitizens, the Sioux's rights as individuals had been limited and their voice feeble. Although they were at first uncertain how to utilize this new citizenship, it would prove significant in the future. Once again, they had shown their adaptability and, as a result, reaped unforeseen benefits. By fighting in the white man's war, they had forced him to see them as people, not savages. The eyes of the nation were opening.

Two years later, in 1926, a special task force investigated the reservation conditions. Their report of the poverty endured by these citizens horrified much of the nation. In 1934 the Indian Reorganization Act (IRA) was passed. There was much that was good about this legislation. It ended the practice of allotments, and some of the lost lands were returned. It restored the Indians' freedom of religion. Education and medicine were improved. The old ways, where not completely lost, were revived.

The IRA was not unflawed, however. It also altered the Sioux political structure. No longer would decisions affecting the tribe be considered by a council of elders. Members of an elected tribal council would determine policy. If dishonest tribal members were elected to the tribal council, they could pursue and enact programs of benefit to themselves, not the tribe. In this respect, the IRA promoted factionalism, which is a splitting of the tribe into separate groups, or factions. Typically, tribal factions consist of the traditionalists, who advocate a return to the old ways, and the progressives, who advocate partial assimilation. Nevertheless, the IRA allowed the traditionalists to take one more step toward adaptability, not assimilation, by restoring to them the right to practice the old ways in their new environment.

Red Power

The next phase in the Sioux's ongoing evolution was the most extraordinary. It will be remembered that the Sioux are an ethnocentric people, a people who believe that their culture is the only correct one. In the 1960s, however, the Sioux realized that alone they were not strong enough to initiate necessary changes in government policy and national attitudes. Despite the IRA, reservation conditions remained deplorable. Stronger action was required, and the Sioux could no longer afford the luxury of ethnocentricity. They began to add their voice and their anger to the many Native American organizations founded in the mid–twentieth century.

These organizations were dedicated to improving the lot of the Native Americans, and most of them had at least a few Sioux among their membership. They used the law to enforce old treaties, citizenship rights to vote in favorable legislation, and politics to push through change, lobbying Congress for bills beneficial to the Native Americans. They also used political activism techniques, such as the occupation of Alcatraz Island in 1969, which was sponsored by the group Indians of All Nations, to protest past treaty violations. Most favored the use of peaceful methods as the most effective means of promoting change. In 1968, however, an Indian activist group was founded that would, in the early 1970s, explode into violence: the American Indian Movement (AIM).

Interestingly, AIM was founded by the traditional Sioux enemy, the Ojibwa, the same tribe responsible for the Sioux's unfortunate name. It is ironic that, of all the countless Native American organizations to arise during the troubled 1960s, this is the one that would most appeal to the Sioux. Then again, maybe it is less ironic and more demonstrative of yet another step taken in their evolutionary journey. A strong desire to improve the lifestyle of subsequent generations replaced the old ethnocentric ways. The Sioux could not

In an attempt to make the plight of Native Americans known to the general public, Indians of All Nations occupied Alcatraz in 1969.

hope to enact change if they bore a grudge against the Ojibwa or their other traditional enemies. They were quick to jump on the AIM bandwagon. In her book *Lakota Woman*, Mary Crow Dog writes, "The American Indian Movement hit our reservation like a tornado, like a new wind blowing out of nowhere, a drumbeat from far off getting louder and louder. It was almost like the Ghost Dance fever that had hit the tribes in 1890 . . . spreading like a prairie fire."[59]

AIM began with high ideals. Its members, radical traditionalists, had found yet another white man's method to use against him: the media, primarily the television journalists who cover newsworthy events. Many Sioux youths joined AIM, traveling across the country together and using the media to draw the nation's attention to wrongs. They protested the callous unearthing of old Indian graves for the construction of shopping malls or for anthropological displays. They attended the political trials of fellow Native Americans, where they picketed and sounded the drums. And, in the words of Crow Dog, "Wherever we saw a bar with a sign NO INDIANS ALLOWED, we sensitized the owners, sometimes quite forcefully."[60]

Wounded Knee Revisited

Somewhere along the way, AIM had lost sight of peaceful objectives. Leadership shifted to those advocating more forceful methods of achieving change. Experience taught them that the media preferred violent demonstrations to those of a more peaceful nature. In late winter of 1973 this new attitude combined with an ugly set of circumstances to explode into violence. The Oglala Pine Ridge tribal council had come under the control of a progressive, Richard Wilson. Wilson was strongly disliked by the traditionalists, and for good reason. He had a particularly nasty way of enforcing council policy, which was allegedly favorable to his personal needs. When anyone crossed Wilson, he called out his GOONs (Guardians of the Oglala Nation), who took care of the offender by violent methods, even murdering the most vocal. Wilson did not like AIM. Reservation life suited Wilson, and he was determined to resist change.

When Pine Ridge AIM members returned to the reservation after their latest protest, having recently occupied the BIA offices in Washington, D.C., "Richard Wilson and his backers met them with a gauntlet of intimidation,"[61] writes David Hurst Thomas. The Lakota AIM members had to make a quick decision. Should they allow themselves to be intimidated or should they make a stand? And, if making a stand was the right thing to do, where should that stand be made? The obvious choice, given AIM's practice of media utilization, was a site fraught with symbolism, one familiar to both Indians and whites: Wounded Knee.

On February 27, 1973, according to Thomas, AIM "seized the trading post and Catholic church in the reservation town of Wounded Knee, South Dakota."[62] In so doing, they brought down upon themselves

The Sioux in Film

From the onset of the movie and television industries, the Indian has been portrayed in an unrealistic and occasionally uncomplimentary manner. Because most non-Indians base their opinion of Indians on those they view in the film media, the Sioux are reduced to a stereotype. This stereotype is beautifully described by Richard Erdoes in his book *The Sun Dance People.*

"Several generations of white children have grown up with the image of a small, heroic band of whites successfully standing up to hoards of feathered fiends. The Indians made it easy for their enemies by riding stupidly around and around the whites until they were all shot dead. If there were too many Indians, the cavalry came to the rescue. As the bugle sounded the charge, hundreds of little white hands would clap in glee, but not even the well-known bugle call was authentic."

More than the authenticity of the bugle call was in question. Despite significant intertribal differences in dress, most of these Indians dressed the same, no matter the region. The actors were often whites, such as Victor Mature, wearing bronze face makeup. Sometimes the extras were Indians in desperate need of employment.

Recent decades have seen a change in this stereotype. Two movies in particular have made great strides toward presenting an accurate portrayal of the Sioux, both past and present. In 1990 Kevin Costner starred in and directed the critically acclaimed *Dances with Wolves,* a tale about post–Civil War Indian–United States relations. The year 1992 saw the release of Tri Star Pictures' *Thunderheart,* starring Val Kilmer as an FBI agent who comes to terms with his Sioux ancestry. Because of films of this nature, the old stereotypes are rapidly becoming a thing of the past.

the wrath of not only Wilson and his GOONs but also of the FBI. For seventy-one days AIM members held Wounded Knee, conducting traditional religious ceremonies when not shooting it out with the federal government. During that time, two Native Americans were killed, one a Lakota, and several others were wounded. There was also a baby born to Mary Crow Dog, symbolic perhaps of the rebirth of the Lakota spirit. One hundred and twenty AIM members were arrested when the confrontation ended, but the endeavor was not considered a failure. The eyes of the nation had turned once again to the Sioux.

Reservation Conditions

Although many people believed that the tactics used to generate this awareness were excessive, a like amount wondered why such excess was necessary. A closer look was taken at reservations, and many Americans were appalled to learn about the poverty, racism, and depression endured by their inhabitants. The Sioux are confined to over a dozen reservations, most of these in the state of South Dakota. At the time of the AIM occupation of Wounded Knee, conditions on these reservations remained some of the worst in the United States. Per capita income for the state of South Dakota was, and still is, invariably the lowest in the nation, primarily because of the poverty endured by the reservation Sioux, who are limited in their employment opportunities. Much of the tribal land is leased to non-Sioux ranchers, and there are few major business concerns offering employment in commercial ventures.

When these men and women seek employment off of the reservation, however, they occasionally encounter racism. Although their numbers are few—in the 1970s the large Oglala Pine Ridge Reservation boasted only twenty thousand residents—it is not uncommon for non-Indian citizens in reservation states like South Dakota to automatically assume "Indian" when hearing of crimes involving domestic abuse and/or alcohol. There is a tendency in humans to judge the whole by the part, in this case, to judge all Sioux by the actions of a few. This tendency, known as stereotyping, is the cause of all racism.

Members of the American Indian Movement (AIM) during their 1973 stand at Wounded Knee.

Frustrated by their inability to support their families, forced to rely on federal welfare programs, and confronted with racism, their self-esteem suffers, often leading to an overwhelming sense of depression.

In addition to this, they have to deal with the encroachment of irresponsible non-Sioux businesses. In the summer of 1962, a uranium mill in Edgemont, South Dakota, spilled over two hundred tons of uranium waste into the Cheyenne River, which runs along the northwestern boundary of the Pine Ridge Reservation. Later analyses of Cheyenne River water samples showed that the radioactivity levels were three times those deemed life-threatening by the federal government. Seventeen years later, the effects of this spillage were still being felt. In the words of author Winona LaDuke,

A preliminary study of 1979 reported that fourteen women, or thirty-eight percent of the pregnant women on the Pine Ridge reservation miscarried. . . . Of the children who were born, some sixty to seventy percent suffered from breathing complications as a result of undeveloped lungs and/or jaundice. Some were born with such birth defects as cleft palate and club foot. . . . Between 1971 and 1979, 314 babies had been born with birth defects, in a total Indian population of under 20,000.[63]

Admittedly, alcoholism perhaps contributed to some of these birth defects.

Children born to alcoholic mothers can suffer from fetal alcohol syndrome, a debilitating disease that results in varying degrees of mental retardation or early death. Often depression at their inability to support their families leads Sioux men and women to turn to alcohol, itself a depressant. This in turn may contribute to the frequency of incidents of domestic abuse. All told, one thing led to another, each forcing the Sioux to tread a vicious circle. In 1990 Crow Dog described the contemporary Sioux warrior as follows:

As for being warriors, the only way some men can count coup nowadays is knocking out another skin's [Sioux's] teeth during a barroom fight. In the old days a man made a name for himself by being generous and wise, but now he has nothing to be generous with, no jobs, no money; and as far as our traditional wisdom is concerned, our men are being told by the white missionaries, teachers, and employers that it is merely savage superstition they should get rid of if they want to make it in this world. . . . So some warriors come home drunk and beat up their old ladies in order to work off their frustration.[64]

An Ongoing Evolution

Unemployment, racism, dangerous environmental conditions, alcoholism, domestic abuse, and the loss or harm of precious children would be more than many soci-

Indian gaming has benefitted many tribes by creating jobs, increasing revenue, and reducing welfare needs.

eties could bear. However, the Sioux's history is one of adaptability under adverse circumstances. The evolution from despair to pride is ongoing. The Sioux are continuing to use the white man's methods to improve their current lifestyle. Interestingly, their past efforts to generate awareness have paid off in new attitudes, considerably lightening the uphill climb. Today, many non-Sioux are as concerned as the Sioux about reservation conditions, which makes change easier to achieve. One example of this can be seen in the introduction of gambling to Sioux reservations. "Sixty-eight percent of Americans polled in a national survey . . . support casino gambling on Indian reservations for reasons including job creation, state revenue, welfare reduction,"[65] according to writer Tim Johnson. In the 1990s the Sioux took advantage of this support, opening several casinos. The inhabitants of South Dakota and Minnesota now flock to lose their money in Sioux casinos.

The Indian Gaming Regulatory Act, enacted in 1988, specifies that funds generated by these casinos be earmarked for tribal programs. If the tribe is able to satisfy certain guidelines, however, profits may be divided between individual tribal members. In fact, a small 250-member band of Dakota Mdewakantons has established three casinos that serve as models of this distribution. Its tribal members live comfortably off the tribe's casino proceeds, and other Native Americans are studying their methods before setting up their own casinos. Additionally, Sioux casinos hire Sioux employees, so there are increased employment opportunities within reservation boundaries.

The Sioux have also learned of the profit to be gained on tourism, one of South Dakota's primary industries, selling their arts and crafts to the millions of U.S. citizens who visit the state each year. They continue to push through federal programs beneficial to their people, such as the Aid

The Native American Church

The twentieth century brought a new religion to the Sioux. In the latter part of the nineteenth century, the half-Comanche Quanah Parker became deathly ill while visiting his white relatives. When it appeared he would die, his relatives obeyed his request that an Indian healer be called. This healer, a Mexican woman, cured Parker by praying and smoking over him and offering him a tea so bitter he could barely keep it down. Within days Parker had made a miraculous recovery. Determined to learn the woman's magic, Parker pestered her for instruction in her ways. Thus was born the Native American Church, also known as the Peyote Cult.

This religion, a combination of Christianity and native beliefs, centers on a cactus bud called peyote. Peyote possesses mildly hallucinogenic properties, and when ingested, it can give the participant visions. However, the rituals of the Native American Church consist of much more than eating a cactus bud or drinking of its tea.

There is a special ceremony to be followed, an all-night ritual of prayer, song, and pipe smoking around a specially prepared altar. Numerous other paraphernalia are also involved: mescal beads, jewelry, sticks held by the priest responsible for officiating at the ceremony, and cedar, which is burnt as a form of incense. Quanah Parker introduced several tribes to the Peyote Cult, and representatives of most Native American tribes are now active members.

The Sioux adopted the Native American Church in the 1920s. It is now estimated that as many as one-third of Sioux tribal members participate in peyote meetings. However, the Peyote Cult has not replaced the old religion. There are still sun dances, vision quests, and purification rites. The rituals of the Native American Church merely provide one more way for the Sioux to worship Wakan Tanka, with the peyote providing a new means of communicating with this deity.

to Dependent Children (ADC) program, which helps single mothers. Perhaps most importantly, they have begun to take charge of their own education, beginning with the establishment of tribal colleges.

In 1971 Oglala Lakota College was established on the Pine Ridge Reservation. Then a two-year college, it now offers a master's degree in Lakota leadership. In 1973 Sinte Gleska Junior College on the Rosebud Sioux Reservation, operating under a board of directors solely composed of Indians, awarded its first two-year degree. By 1989 Sinte Gleska, now a university, was awarding master's degrees in elementary education. Because of this, the Sioux are now able to educate their own children. Reservation schools have replaced boarding schools, and graduates of Sinte Gleska's master's program in education generally choose to utilize their degrees at these schools. Many Sioux children are no longer taught by non-Sioux instructors, nor are they compelled to assume non-Sioux customs. Furthermore, the curriculum at these schools, while meeting national standards, includes courses geared to the Sioux heritage.

Tribal coffers fattened by gambling and tourist dollars, increased employment opportunities, federal programs geared toward aiding the poor, and reservation-educated children and young adults—this is only the beginning. The century-long evolution is ongoing. The ancestors of the contemporary Sioux took two centuries to evolve from poor woodland Indians to mighty Great Plains warriors. Today's warriors, both men and women, have another century to complete the desired change, to court adaptability while resisting assimilation. Given their history, it is not unreasonable to perceive their future with a healthy dose of optimism.

Notes

Introduction: A Migration from the Woods of Minnesota to the Upper Great Plains

1. Francis Parkman, *La Salle and the Discovery of the Great West.* Williamstown, MA: Corner House, 1968, p. 6.
2. John Upton Terrell, *Sioux Trail.* New York: McGraw-Hill, 1974, pp. 187–88.

Chapter 1: Life on "the Great American Desert"

3. Alvin M. Josephy Jr., *The Indian Heritage of America.* New York: Knopf, 1968, p. 111.
4. Terrell, *Sioux Trail,* p. 192.
5. Royal B. Hassrick, *The Sioux: Life and Customs of a Warrior Society.* Norman: University of Oklahoma Press, 1964, p. 171.
6. Norman Bancroft-Hunt, *The Indians of the Great Plains.* New York: Peter Bedrick Books, 1989, p. 52.
7. Bancroft-Hunt, *The Indians of the Great Plains,* p. 53.
8. Bancroft-Hunt, *The Indians of the Great Plains,* p. 52.
9. Hassrick, *The Sioux,* p. 177.
10. Hassrick, *The Sioux,* p. 177.

Chapter 2: Dogs of War: The Horse and a Culture Based on War

11. George E. Hyde, *Red Cloud's Folk.* Norman: University of Oklahoma Press, 1937, p. 18.
12. Hyde, *Red Cloud's Folk,* p. 20.
13. Samuel Sidney, *The Book of the Horse.* New York: Crown, 1985, p. 147.
14. Quoted in Frank Gilbert Roe, *The Indian and His Horse.* Norman: University of Oklahoma Press, 1955, p. 119.
15. Hassrick, *The Sioux,* p. 185.
16. Josephy, *The Indian Heritage of America,* p. 118.
17. Robert West Howard, *The Horse in America.* Chicago: Follett, 1965, pp. 91–92.
18. Hassrick, *The Sioux,* p. 15.
19. Hyde, *Red Cloud's Folk,* p. 32.
20. Hyde, *Red Cloud's Folk,* p. 32.
21. Quoted in Roe, *The Indian and His Horse,* p. 193.

Chapter 3: Social and Political Organization: The Individual, the Band, the Tribe

22. Bancroft-Hunt, *The Indians of the Great Plains,* p. 45.

23. Bancroft-Hunt, *The Indians of the Great Plains,* p. 45.

24. Hassrick, *The Sioux,* pp. 13–14.

25. Bancroft-Hunt, *The Indians of the Great Plains,* p. 48.

26. Hassrick, *The Sioux,* p. 21.

27. Hassrick, *The Sioux,* p. 17.

28. Hassrick, *The Sioux,* pp. 16–17.

29. Hassrick, *The Sioux,* p. 27.

30. Vine Deloria Jr., *Custer Died for Your Sins: An Indian Manifesto.* London: Collier-Macmillan, 1969, pp. 3–4.

Chapter 4: Customs and Religion: In Worship of Wakan Tanka

31. James R. Walker, *Lakota Society,* ed. Raymond J. DeMallie. Lincoln: University of Nebraska Press, 1982, pp. 54–55.

32. Walker, *Lakota Society,* p. 55.

33. Ruth M. Underhill, *Red Man's Religion: Beliefs and Practices of the Indians North of Mexico.* Chicago: University of Chicago Press, 1972, pp. 79–80.

34. Terrell, *Sioux Trail,* p. 188.

35. Black Elk, *The Sacred Pipe: Black Elk's Account of the Seven Rites of the Oglala Sioux,* ed. Joseph Epes Brown. Norman: University of Oklahoma Press, 1975, p. 69.

36. Underhill, *Red Man's Religion,* p. 79.

37. Black Elk, *The Sacred Pipe,* p. 43.

38. Black Elk, *The Sacred Pipe,* p. 46.

39. Black Elk, *The Sacred Pipe,* p. 67.

40. Hyde, *Red Cloud's Folks,* pp. 41–42.

Chapter 5: The White Man Cometh: From Fur Traders to the Settlers

41. Reuben Gold Thwaites, ed., *Original Journals of the Lewis and Clark Expedition, 1804–1806,* vol. 6. New York: Arno, 1969, p. 98.

42. Thwaites, *Original Journals of the Lewis and Clark Expedition, 1804-1806,* p. 95.

43. David J. Wishart, *The Fur Trade of the American West, 1807–1840: A Geographical Synthesis.* Lincoln: University of Nebraska Press, 1992, p. 214.

44. Terrell, *Sioux Trail,* p. 176.

45. Hyde, *Red Cloud's Folks,* p. 116.

46. Ralph K. Andrist, *The Long Death: The Last Days of the Plains Indians.* New York: Macmillan, 1964, p. 265.

47. Angie Debo, *A History of the Indians of the United States.* Norman: University of Oklahoma Press, 1979, p. 238.

Chapter 6: Elimination of "Siouxness": Confinement to Reservations

48. Robert M. Utley, *The Indian Frontier of the American West: 1846–1890.* Albuquerque: University of New Mexico Press, 1984, p. 229.

49. David Hurst Thomas et al., *The Native Americans: An Illustrated History.* Atlanta: Turner, 1993, p. 360.

50. Debo, *A History of the Indians of the United States,* p. 304.

51. Debo, *A History of the Indians of the United States,* p. 290.

52. Andrist, *The Long Death,* p. 337.

53. Andrist, *The Long Death,* p. 350.

54. Andrist, *The Long Death,* p. 351.

55. Debo, *A History of the Indians of the United States,* p. 293.

56. Thomas, *The Native Americans,* p. 427.

57. Josephy, *The Indian Heritage of America,* p. 353.

**Chapter 7: A New Evolution:
Adaptation to Their New Environment**

58. Josephy, *The Indian Heritage of America,* p. 351.

59. Mary Crow Dog and Richard Erdoes, *Lakota Woman.* New York: Grove Weidenfeld, 1990, p. 73.

60. Crow Dog and Erdoes, *Lakota Woman,* p. 79.

61. Thomas, *The Native Americans,* p. 440.

62. Thomas, *The Native Americans,* p. 440.

63. Quoted in Susan Lobo and Steve Talbot, *Native American Voices: A Reader.* New York: Longman, 1998, p. 320.

64. Crow Dog and Erdoes, *Lakota Woman,* p. 5.

65. Quoted in Lobo and Talbot, *Native American Voices,* p. 348.

For Further Reading

Nancy Bonvillain, *The Santee Sioux*. Philadelphia: Chelsea House, 1997. A little dry, but takes a good look at the traditions, history, and current lifestyle of the Dakota.

———, *The Teton Sioux*. New York: Chelsea House, 1994. Somewhat top-heavy in political history, but overall a good account of the Lakota.

Vinson Brown, *Great upon the Mountain*. New York: Macmillan, 1971. A biography of the Oglala leader Crazy Horse told in story form from the Sioux point of view.

Benjamin Capps, *The Great Chiefs*. Alexandria, VA: Time-Life Books, 1975. Covers several Native American leaders, including an excellent biography of Sitting Bull.

———, *The Indians*. Alexandria, VA: Time-Life Books, 1979. Primarily a Plains Indians history. Very interesting and readable.

Richard Erdoes, *The Sun Dance People*. New York: Knopf, 1972. Excellent treatment of the Plains Indians with an emphasis on recent history and the Lakota. The best of the Plains Indians books.

Royal B. Hassrick, *The Colorful Story of the American West*. London: Octopus Books, 1975. Not a lot about the Sioux, but nonetheless a highly entertaining account of the white invasion. Nicely illustrated.

Robert Hofsinde (Gray-Wolf), *The Indian Medicine Man*. New York: William Morrow, 1966. An easy-reading, informative book on the spiritual practices of six different tribes, including the Sioux.

Herbert T. Hoover, *The Yankton Sioux*. New York: Chelsea House, 1988. An objective treatment of the Yankton history with an emphasis on the reservation years.

Francis Parkman, *The Oregon Trail*. New York: Rinehart, 1931. An entertaining, well-written account of the author's nineteenth-century sojourn along the Oregon Trail. He spent much of his time in the company of the Sioux and has a number of insights to offer regarding their customs. For the middle-level reader.

Marian T. Place, *Westward on the Oregon Trail.* New York: American Heritage, 1962. Illustrated. Only a small portion is dedicated to the Sioux, but it gives a good idea of what they were up against regarding the white invasion of their territory.

Mari Sandoz, *Crazy Horse: The Strange Man of the Oglalas.* Lincoln: University of Nebraska Press, 1961. A biography of Crazy Horse told in story tale form from the Sioux point of view. Generally considered the most readable of the Crazy Horse biographies.

Websites

Cheyenne River Sioux Tribe (www.sioux.org). One of the more extensive websites, information can be found on the history, Tribal Council, geographical location, the Cheyenne River Sioux flag, hunting and fishing, and the Lakota campus of Presentation College.

Rosebud Sioux Tribe (www.rosebudsiouxtribe.org). This website offers information on the tribal council and programs of the Rosebud Sioux tribe.

Sisseton-Wahpeton Sioux Tribe (www.swcc.cc.sd.us). Maintained by students at the Sisseton Wahpeton Community College, this website offers information on upcoming events, Dakota history and culture, and Dakota arts and language.

South Dakota State Department of Tourism (www.state.sd/state/executive/tourism.sioux). Many of the Sioux tribes are addressed in this tourism-generated website.

Standing Rock Sioux Tribe (www.indian.com/srst). Includes information on the government, land, people, culture, and history of the Standing Rock Sioux tribe.

Works Consulted

Ralph K. Andrist, *The Long Death: The Last Days of the Plains Indians*. New York: Macmillan, 1964. Detailed coverage of the Great Plains wars, from the 1862 Santee uprising to the massacre at Wounded Knee.

Norman Bancroft-Hunt, *The Indians of the Great Plains*. New York: Peter Bedrick Books, 1989. The text may be a little advanced for younger readers, but the illustrations are worth a look.

Louise Barry, *The Beginning of the West: Annals of the Kansas Gateway to the American West, 1540–1854*. Topeka: Kansas State Historical Society, 1972. A reference to documents relating to the settlement of the West.

Black Elk, *The Sacred Pipe: Black Elk's Account of the Seven Rites of the Oglala Sioux*. Ed. Joseph Epes Brown. Norman: University of Oklahoma Press, 1975. There is no better or more readable treatment of the Lakota religion available. For the serious student of Sioux religion.

Helen H. Blish, *A Pictographic History of the Oglala Sioux*. Lincoln: University of Nebraska Press, 1967. An invaluable collection of the four-hundred-plus pictographs prepared by Oglala Amos Bad Heart Bull from 1890 until his death in 1913, with an explanatory text by the author.

Dee Brown, *Bury My Heart at Wounded Knee*. New York: Henry Holt, 1991. A lengthy account of the injustices suffered by Native Americans throughout the history of the United States.

Mary Crow Dog and Richard Erdoes, *Lakota Woman*. New York: Grove Weidenfeld, 1990. Mary Crow Dog was an active player in AIM, giving birth to her first son during the 1973 siege of Wounded Knee. Although blunt at times, with explicit profanities, this book is well worth a read by the advanced reader.

Angie Debo, *A History of the Indians of the United States.* Norman: University of Oklahoma Press, 1979. Thoroughly and concisely articulates Native American history from the arrival of the first explorers through the reservation years.

Vine Deloria Jr., *Custer Died for Your Sins: An Indian Manifesto.* London: Collier-Macmillan, 1969. The author, a Standing Rock Sioux, gives the Indian perspective on government policy and errors.

Frances Densmore, *Teton Sioux Music.* Washington, DC: Government Printing Office, 1918. Financed by the Bureau of American Ethnology, this book contains the most extensive collection of Teton (and Crow) songs available, with an informative, albeit highly technical, explanatory text.

Richard Erdoes, *Crying for a Dream.* Santa Fe, NM: Bear, 1989. An explanation of Native American religious ceremonies practiced by the Sioux and some other Plains tribes.

Royal B. Hassrick, *The Sioux: Life and Customs of a Warrior Society.* Norman: University of Oklahoma Press, 1964. The most comprehensive treatment available of the Sioux's religious, political, and social customs.

Robert West Howard, *The Horse in America.* Chicago: Follett, 1965. A fascinating account of the American horse, from eohippus to the establishment of American breeds to their fall from favor in the industrial era.

George E. Hyde, *Red Cloud's Folks.* Norman: University of Oklahoma Press, 1937. Perhaps the most authoritative account of the Oglala, from their golden years to their decline.

Alvin M. Josephy Jr., *The Indian Heritage of America.* New York: Knopf, 1968. Broad treatment of the Native Americans intended to present a pragmatic, romance-dispelling picture.

Reginald and Gladys Laubin, *Indian Dances of North America: Their Importance to Indian Life.* Norman: University of Oklahoma Press, 1977. A detailed account of ceremonial dance written by adopted members of the Lakota tribe.

Susan Lobo and Steve Talbot, *Native American Voices: A Reader.* New York: Longman, 1998. An anthology of articles addressing contemporary issues affecting Native Americans.

Thomas E. Mails, *Plains Indians: Dog Soldiers, Bear Men, and Buffalo Women.* New York: Bonanza Books, 1985. Advanced text depicting the social fraternities of the Plains tribes, superbly illustrated with sketches by the author.

Alice Marriot and Carol K. Rachlin, *Peyote.* New York: Thomas Y. Crowell, 1971. A history and description of the Native American Church.

Larry McMurtry, *Crazy Horse.* New York: Penguin Putnam, 1999. More a rambling history of the Sioux wars than a biography of Crazy Horse.

John G. Neihardt, *Black Elk Speaks.* Lincoln: University of Nebraska Press, 1988. A history of Oglala holy man Black Elk as told to the author.

Francis Parkman, *La Salle and the Discovery of the Great West.* Williamstown, MA: Corner House, 1968. A book centering on the experiences of the first fur traders and trappers and the first missionaries. Not Parkman's most readable book.

Frank Gilbert Roe, *The Indian and His Horse.* Norman: University of Oklahoma Press, 1955. From the Indians' first encounter with the horse in the fifteenth century to its use in the last Indian wars, this book covers the horse's dissemination, husbandry in Indian hands, and influence.

Samuel Sidney, *The Book of the Horse.* New York: Crown, 1985. A Classic Edition reprint of the 1880s original, this book addresses nineteenth-century breeds, equipment, uses, and husbandry.

Colin F. Taylor, *The Plains Indians.* New York: Crescent Books, 1994. Another illustrated overview of the Plains tribes with occasionally difficult text but excellent illustrations.

John Upton Terrell, *Sioux Trail.* New York: McGraw-Hill, 1974. A well-written prehistory account of all tribes linked by the Siouan language, with brief references to both customs and respective nineteenth-century conflicts.

David Hurst Thomas et al., *The Native Americans: An Illustrated History.* Atlanta: Turner, 1993. A broad treatment of all Indian tribes from speculation about their origins to speculation about their future. Nicely illustrated with often fascinating sidebars.

Reuben Gold Thwaites, ed., *Original Journals of the Lewis and Clark Expedition, 1804–1806.* Vol. 6. New York: Arno, 1969. Includes the meticulously kept journals of Meriwether Lewis and William Rogers Clark during their exploration of the Louisiana Territory and the Pacific Northwest, as well as the journals of other members of the parties, and their correspondence with Washington, D.C.

Ruth M. Underhill, *Red Man's Religion: Beliefs and Practices of the Indians North of Mexico.* Chicago: University of Chicago Press, 1972. Discusses the religious customs, traditions, and ceremonies of a number of tribes, including the Sioux.

Robert M. Utley, *The Indian Frontier of the American West: 1846–1890.* Albuquerque: University of New Mexico Press, 1984. Covers government Indian policy throughout the wars for the Great Plains from 1846 to 1890, from the beginnings of the westward movement to the confinement of all tribes to reservations.

James R. Walker, *Lakota Society.* Ed. Raymond J. DeMallie. Lincoln: University of Nebraska Press, 1982. Primary accounts of Sioux customs collected by the author during an eighteen-year stint at the Pine Ridge Reservation from 1896 to 1914.

David J. Wishart, *The Fur Trade of the American West, 1807–1840: A Geographical Synthesis.* Lincoln: University of Nebraska Press, 1992. A thorough treatment of the early American, French, and British fur trade, including its internal machinery and its influence on the Native Americans.

Clark Wissler, *Indians of the United States.* New York: Doubleday, 1966. One of the more readable histories of the Native Americans, from the first explorers and colonists to the reservation years.

Websites

Oglala Lakota College (www.olc.edu). Oglala Lakota College was one of the first two Sioux-operated reservation colleges. This website includes, among other things, its mission statement and history.

Sinte Gleska University (www.sinte.indian.com). A history of Sinte Gleska University, one of the few Native American universities to offer a master's in education. Fascinating information on the Brule leader Spotted Tail, for whom the university is named.

Index

Picture Credits

Cover photo: © The Newberry Library/Stock Montage, Inc.
Archive Photos, 31, 33, 53, 54
Corbis, 10, 37, 89
Corbis-Bettmann, 87
Golden Gate National Park Recreation Area, 84
Library of Congress, 28, 29, 61, 64, 66, 77
Minnesota Historical Society, 41
National Archive, 62, 74, 79
New York Public Library, 14
North Wind Picture Archives, 16, 19, 20, 24, 51
Prints Old & Rare, 73
South Dakota State Historical Society, 69
Stock Montage, Inc., 27, 39, 59

About the Author

Gwen Remington, a native of North Dakota, has published fiction and nonfiction pieces in several horse magazines. In 1997 she graduated magna cum laude from the University of Sioux Falls, earning her bachelors degree in English. In 1998 she obtained her master's degree, also in English. Although Ms. Remington has lived in South Dakota for most of her adult life, she currently resides in Cheyenne, Wyoming, where she is working on her first novel.